PRISONER: CELL BLOCK H

Other Books by Terry Bourke

CROCODILE (with Olaf Ruhen) 1979
LITTLE BOY LOST (with Olaf Ruhen) 1980
STARS OF HOME AND AWAY 1988

About the Author

Terry Bourke is Australia's most prolific showbiz writer, having been a chronicler and participant in his country's TV since its introduction in 1956, and a prominent member of the film industry from the early 1970s renaissance. He has written, directed or produced eight movies and more than 700 hours of television drama, comedy and sport and written columns for all the major media owners Down Under, directing many of the top Australian actors and actresses or meeting them as a working journalist. He has also tutored more than 1,000 classes in scripting and film and TV production in Australia, Hong Kong and Hawaii.

PRISONER: CELL BLOCK H

BEHIND THE SCENES

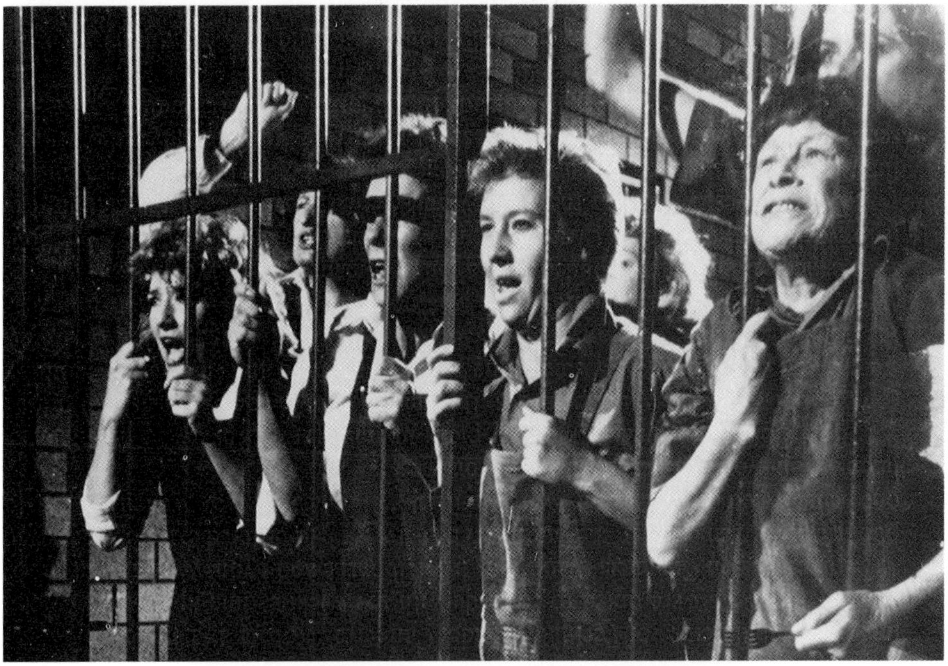

TERRY BOURKE

ANGUS & ROBERTSON

A division of HarperCollins *Publishers*

For Bob Gordon and Ben Mitchell,
the last two maverick TV editors in Australia.
They don't breed 'em any more . . .

Acknowledgements

Special thanks to all the fine folk at News Ltd, Sydney – Warren Beeby, Peter Wylie, photo librarian Dell Courtney, reference librarians Lurline Campbell, John Knight, and my midnight shift mate Clive Powell; Alan Farrelly (founding editor, Sunday Herald, Melbourne); Edith Lesser, photo librarian, Australian Consolidated Press, Sydney; all the guys and gals who worked on 'Prisoner' and gave so much of their time and memories; and their agents, especially Garry Stewart; the 'real' prisoner, Sandra Willson; and Val, in London.

Unless otherwise stated all black and white photographs are reproduced courtesy of News Limited, Sydney, and all colour photographs courtesy of Australian Consolidated Press, Sydney.

AN ANGUS & ROBERTSON BOOK

Angus & Robertson (UK)
16 Golden Square, London, W1R 4BN
United Kingdom
Collins/Angus & Robertson Publishers Australia
A division of HarperCollins Publishers
(Australia) Pty Limited
Unit 4, Eden Park, 31 Waterloo Road,
North Ryde, NSW 2113, Australia
William Collins Publishers Ltd
31 View Road, Glenfield, Auckland 10,
New Zealand

First published in the United Kingdom by
Angus & Robertson (UK) in 1990

Typeset in Great Britain by New Faces, Bedford
Printed by ScotPrint Ltd, Musselburgh, Scotland

British Library Cataloguing in Publication Data
Bourke, Terry
Prisoner Cell Block H: behind the scenes.
1. Television drama series in English
I. Title
791.45

ISBN 0 207 16873 3

CONTENTS

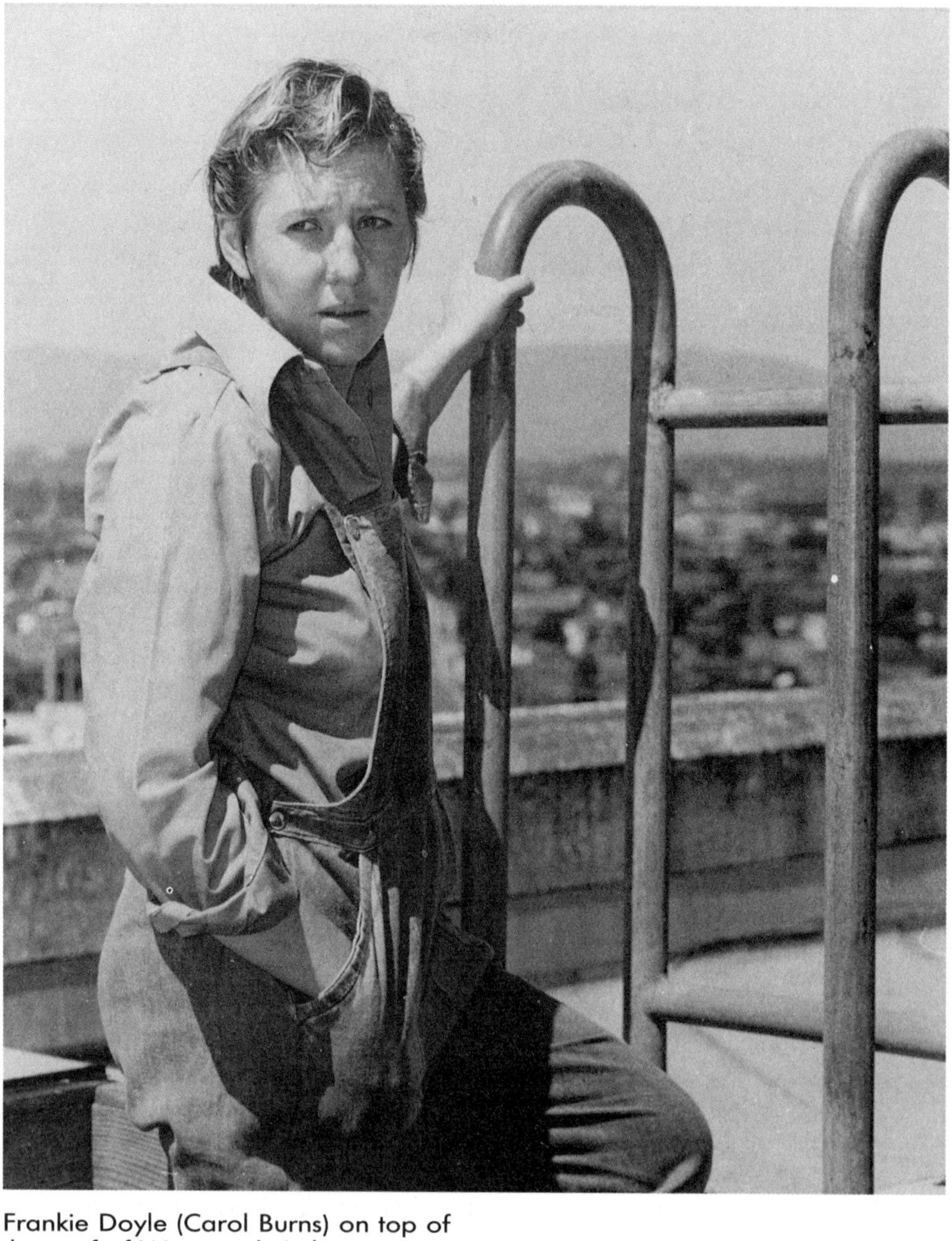

Frankie Doyle (Carol Burns) on top of the roof of Wentworth Jail, surveying the beckoning free world outside ... she makes the decision to break out of her hell-hole

1

PROLOGUE: THE BEGINNINGS OF A CULT

The security guard at KTLA-5 couldn't believe his eyes. Outside on Hollywood's famous Sunset Boulevard were about twenty women motor-bike riders converging near the footpath in front of the TV station's main offices. Engines revved and roared. The din was ear-splitting. As a colleague joined the guard behind the glass panelling in the foyer, fifteen more women bikies rode in from a nearby carpark, then another fifteen arced in from the opposite direction. The two guards moved to the front door, prepared to disperse the assembly of fifty gleaming machines and their leather-clad riders. The men stopped in their tracks. Now there was an eerie calm. The bikies sat silently, heads down in reverent prayer. Passers-by, accustomed to bizarre events every day and night on Sunset Strip, seemed to sense the occasion and stood still in tribute. It looked like a scene from the classic 1953 Marlon Brando movie *The Wild One*. But this was Los Angeles, and it was 10 January 1980. The bikies were paying respect to their favourite TV character Franky Doyle, a trouble-making lesbian bikie inmate of the fictitious Wentworth Jail in an offbeat Australian drama series called 'Prisoner: Cell Block H'. The previous night on KTLA-5 Doyle had 'died' from a police bullet while trying to escape. Now a small solitary wreath lay on the sunlit footpath and Doyle (played by actress Carol Burns) was being paid homage in a manner Hollywood usually reserves for its own dead cult heroes and heroines like Rudolf Valentino, Marilyn Monroe, James Dean and Elvis Presley. Then the bikies were moving off in a slow, orderly line, light on the accelerators as their gleaming, mechanical caravan headed off into the hazy shroud of another Los Angeles morning. Across town other bikie groups of Franky Doyle fans would swell the ranks at official wakes to more than 3,000. Only once before had Hollywood created an Australian cult hero, the swashbuckling, macho actor Errol Flynn – and he'd been dead for twenty-one years. . . .

2

THE IDEA, THE REALISATION

Reg Watson is one of the most prolific creator-writers of television soap in the world. His output and successes dwarf even the loftiest of American soap or drama originators and he is among several Australian behind-the-scenes TV giants who gained early experience in the best of circles – London's time-honoured TV drama battlefield.

Watson was born in Brisbane, but earned his stripes creating the long-running British ITV series 'Crossroads'. Yet it was back home that his amazing career blossomed as the man behind the avalanche of soaps emanating from the Sydney-based Grundy Organization in the Seventies and Eighties.

The Grundy Organization is a success story unparalleled Down Under. Adelaide-born Reg Grundy, 66, is chairman of a mega-bucks global empire which has established itself as a top-flight programme-maker of drama and game shows – even in the cut-throat world of Hollywood. Grundy, married to actress Joy Chambers, spends much of his time in Bermuda, but is in LA often enough to make sure his office there is up to speed with the main operations in Sydney. There, Reg Watson, is something of a legend. He was the creative force behind the drama shows 'The Restless Years' (1977), 'Case for the Defence' (1977), 'King's Men' (1978). And, of course, 'Neighbours' which followed 'Prisoner' (1979).

'Within These Walls' was a British TV series about a women's prison near London. Googie Withers, a topline veteran actress married to Australian film and TV pioneer actor-producer, John McCallum, presided as the maternal superintendent. It was quite successful and had reasonable exposure around the world. Yet Reg Watson felt it had a major weakness. 'Within These Walls' concentrated on the life of the people who ran the jail. 'There's more interest in the prisoners. They're the crux of a prison series. They provide more varied stories, gutsier situations.' So, while working away on numerous Grundy projects, Watson kept the women's prison show in the back of his mind until the O-TEN network said it was looking for a hard-hitting contemporary series to propel it back into the forefront of local drama – something it had not enjoyed since the halcyon days of the controversial 'Number 96' (1972-76) which took the network from bottom of the heap to top dog ahead of the rival Nine and Seven Networks.

'Number 96's mixture of sex and sin – with outrageous liaisons (Oz TV's first homosexual lovers), the blatant sexual assets of blonde Abigail, the gossiping tenants of the building and a ground-floor delicatessen that seemed to trap even the wariest of passers-by – guaranteed a ratings bonanza and unprecedented national adulation for its string of stars. 'Number 96' had rewritten the history book for Australian home-spun drama and O-TEN desperately wanted to savour again the long-lost taste of success. The time was ripe for the Grundy Organization and Reg Watson's next foray into Oz drama.

Reg Grundy and Ian Holmes (later president of Grundy's) had been discussing the possible success of a women's prison drama since 1977. With 1979 as 'The Year of the Woman', they felt a network should be interested in a strong, contemporary women's drama.

Added impetus came from the extensive media coverage and public awareness at the time of prison issues and, in particular, the status of women inmates in the two main States of New South Wales and Victoria. There had been a riot of gigantic proportions in the rural New South Wales complex, Bathurst Gaol; the highly scrutinised Nagle Royal Commission into N.S.W. prisons in 1976 and 1977; the founding of Women Behind Bars in 1975; and a successful and sustained public campaign for the release of Australia's longest-serving female prisoner, Sandra Willson, who served eighteen years for murder and would become an integral part of the making of the 'Prisoner' series. So, the time for a women's prison drama was right and Grundy's seized the opportunity with both hands.

Reg Grundy is renowned as 'a great ideas man who makes big and quick decisions on gut reaction' – an attribute which has often paid off handsomely for the globe-trotting mogul; Ian Holmes, former boss at Channel Ten (Sydney), where he was instrumental in getting 'Number 96' on air, is held in high esteem for his managerial and 'keeping in touch with viewers' prowess; Watson's record speaks for itself. So the three chiefs at Grundy's were more than quietly confident that their prison show would be an audience-grabber.

The Grundy's brains trust also decided it would only seek out actresses who were not major names or currently in a TV series. This would give the ambitious show a fresh look and create new stars. It would be 'Number 96' all over again!

When they finally gave Watson the go-ahead for development, the eager creator-writer faced nearly a year of research, planning and discussions with writers, key production staff and people in and out of the prison system – including 'the prisoner' Sandra Willson.

Watson freely admits he got more than he bargained for. 'I changed my outlook on prisons and prisoners. The whole thing became a tremendous learning experience.'

The researchers and Watson were not only documenting day-to-day life in a women's prison, but looking for inspirations to create characters, and checking official files for true stories to dramatise. 'We had always planned to use true-life events for the main story lines,' said Watson as the pilot episode took shape on his wordprocessor.

Grundy's were dealing with the Corrective Services Department in New South

Wales and the Victorian Prisons Department in Melbourne, where the series would be taped at the O-TEN Network station in suburban Nunawading. Scores of prisoners, warders, jail bosses and penal reform advocates were interviewed and quizzed over the year of research and planning by the fact-gathering team headed by Peta Letchford.

'There was a need, an obligation, to do it properly. We couldn't just go in and make some fairy-floss story about girls in a weekend camp. This was to be close to the real thing, warts and all. It had a big effect on us,' one of Letchford's team recalled from the early months of jail rounds. 'I had plenty of sleepless nights and some days I dreaded going near the prisons. We heard absolutely horrendous stories from the women prisoners, but were told it was far worse with the men elsewhere.'

It doesn't take much research to learn that, like homosexuality in male prisons, lesbianism is rampant in women's jails. It was obvious to Letchford and her team that

PRISONER FILE

Name: Judy Bryant

Actress: Betty Bobbitt

Lovable lesbian Judy Bryant was a firm favourite with viewers. Actress Betty Bobbitt revealed, 'I got so much mail. At first the letters were from the gay community. Then as Judy changed to show more motherly values, I got letters from all sorts of people who liked her sympathetic nature, including one little girl who asked me to adopt her.'

Judy Bryant is the mainstay of the halfway house outside Wentworth. Based on the experience of Sandra Willson and her halfway house in the Sydney suburb of Enmore, it showed how ex-prisoners could adjust gradually to life beyond bars. 'Meeting Sandra was an incredible experience,' said Betty. 'Any encouragement we can give prisoners by showing the halfway house will be well worthwhile.'

Betty and 'Prisoner' pals Colette Mann and Jane Clifton started singing together to while away the waiting time between shooting and eventually formed a trio, the Mini-Busettes, touring clubs and variety shows.

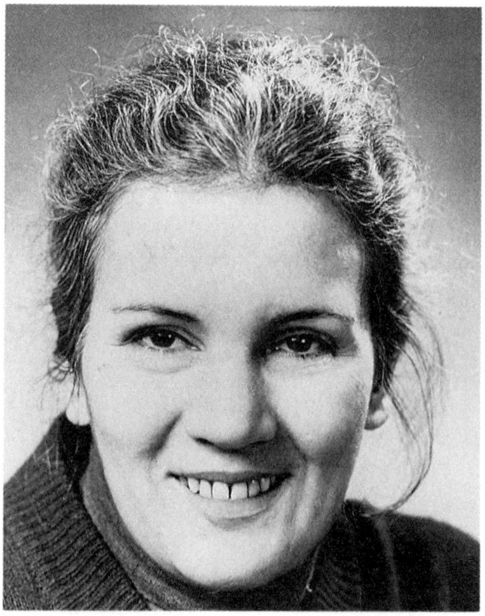

they couldn't pretend it didn't exist or was only practised in dark corners. 'There's sex all over the jails, and we knew that it would be a vital part of the make-up in most of the ruthless characters we would be introducing to viewers in "Prisoner" ' another researcher says. 'Reg (Watson) said we weren't to make major issues about sex, but treat it as part of the routine for inmates and, in some cases, the jail bosses. We were committed to realism, the nitty-gritty – the sex is there, lesbians are there, whatever you can imagine is there. Prisoners get bored and it's either sex or drugs as a diversion – and often both. You want the bottom line on this? Jails are a smorgasbord of sex. "Line up and get it" we were told.'

Initially, the researchers and writers looked at the two main interstate women's jails – Fairlea (Melbourne) and Mulawa (Sydney). But later cast members visited the infamous Pentridge Jail, in the Melbourne suburb of Coburg, scene of the country's last judicial hanging (Ronald Ryan, in 1963). Cop killer William John O'Meally was under sentence of death there for six years from 1952 before his sentence was commuted to life imprisonment, and he was the last inmate to be whipped with the hideous cat-o'-nine-tails (1958).

Pentridge's H–Division houses some of the toughest and worst prisoners, incarcerated under constant supervision and watched by élite, specially-trained guards. Hi-tech video and surveillance equipment watch the inmates' every move. It is a hell-hole for the worst of convicts. Appropriately, 'H' stands for Hell. (Later, 'Prisoner' would be given an added title overseas – 'Cell Block H').

Both Reg Grundy and Ian Holmes had insisted Watson ensure each prisoner's background was explained in the early stages and, where it helped the flow or spiced up proceedings, the crime itself was shown. The series would also show how imprisonment affected the families and friends of the inmates – so the story and cameras could go out of Wentworth Detention Centre, providing respite from the confines of the cells. 'There's good and bad with the inmates and the jailers,' said Watson in one of his earliest interviews for 'Prisoner'. 'We'll show the people who wait for the prisoners, or live with the jailers. We'll show both sides of the coin. It's not just being realistic. It's a matter of being fair. So, we'll go outside Wentworth when necessary. After all, there is life beyond jail.'

3

LOOKING FOR FRANKY, BEA AND VINEGAR TITS

Casting for 'Prisoner' was underway and the ever alert Melbourne and Sydney media tried to zero in on the actresses being sought and auditioned by the Grundy casting boss Kerry Spence and subsequently courted by Reg Watson and producer Ian Bradley. But with near-impregnable security around the assembly of the fledgling cast, the industry and media knew only that a tough prison show was being contemplated by 0-TEN and Grundy's.

Another factor helping Grundy's immeasurably was Holmes and Watson's strict edict to seek experienced stage players, but not necessarily names or faces familiar to the television public. There was to be no general confirmation of cast signings until all roles were settled for the start of shooting on the initial sixteen one-hour episodes in four months' time. And there was no divulging of the potent storyline. Cast and crew were literally under oath not to loan, copy or circulate the scripts.

It was now mid-May 1978. Grundy's had to protect the new stars from unauthorised publicity leaks before all systems were go. And even then there would only be minimal organised publicity permitted.

The Grundy casting net was spread far and wide looking for special faces and talents. Initially, Kerry Spence's spotter teams concentrated on about forty-eight stage shows being performed in theatres in Sydney, Brisbane, Canberra, Melbourne, Adelaide and Perth. There were several great discoveries. 'Prisoner' brought TV stardom to theatre actresses and overdue acclaim to many veteran players. Some actresses who thought their careers had passed them by were swept into the 'Prisoner' whirlpool, swimming ashore with new energies and public recognition.

The subject material made the show potential dynamite and Grundy's couldn't disregard the powerful and inquisitive press. Still, sensational headlines before or during shooting and ahead of the release of the show could mean irresponsible and irreversible controversy about the characters and general theme. There would be official and pressure group outbursts against 'Prisoner'. It was to be expected.

Grundy's concern could be readily gauged just by reading the character breakdown and first scripts: murder *à la* Alfred Hitchcock's *Psycho* shower scene when Anthony Perkins slashed the life out of a naked and defenceless Janet Leigh (only this time a pretty schoolteacher stabs her two-timing husband); suicide; a hanging; assault with a hot iron; an infant buried alive; a tattooed lesbian bikie ruling the roost; and a vicious, vinegary warder who regards violence and fear as the only keys to survival.

Not typical Aussie soap fare. 'Prisoner' was a far cry from its contemporaries, such as 'The Restless Years', about young folk out of school and starting adult life; 'A Country Practice', village and hospital life in a tranquil place called Wandin Valley; 'Carson's Law', the inside stories of legal eagles in the Forties.

It could have been a volatile tabloid blitzkrieg in the wrong hands. Grundy publicists and O-TEN wanted maximum media space further down the track when the series was about to première.

Franky Doyle's character was the hardest to cast. The basic outline said she was a vile, bullying, loud-mouthed, trouble-making tattooed lesbian with a bikie gang background. Violent, destructive and unpredictable – a walking time-bomb! She had been convicted for armed robbery and given nine years in the slammer. Nobody trusted Franky. You got her special kind of message very quickly, and it was the same for the actresses who were approached for the role. They realised instantly it would be one of the most daring and nasty roles on television anywhere in the world. The character would be hated. And the lesbian elements were a major worry for almost every candidate.

Just how many actresses passed on the Franky Doyle offer (or didn't fit the demanding bill) we will never know but there were certainly several, including a couple of famous names. Franky's kinky sex-life frightened most of the potential players. They were reluctant to miss out on the notorious role, and invariably told Watson and Co. they'd be interested – but only if Franky's character was sanitised or made more acceptable.

Looking back it seems obvious only one actress could have portrayed Franky – Carol Burns. Even now, ten years on, Australian audiences can clearly remember Franky. Certainly, Doyle was an oddity, even among the misfits of Wentworth, but few people could have imagined the impact she was to have on viewers in Australia and around the world.

Burns, then 31, was an experienced stage actress from Brisbane. Her biggest role to date had been in the movie *The Mango Tree* (1977), starring American actress Geraldine Fitzgerald, and Australians Sir Robert Helpmann and Christopher Pate, son of the film's director, Michael Pate. At the time, Michael Pate, a seasoned actor-writer-producer, with a wealth of Hollywood credits, had become a welcome fixture in Australian TV circles. He had starred in the series 'Matlock Police' and was a drama consultant to several aspiring producers and helped many writers to polish their scripts.

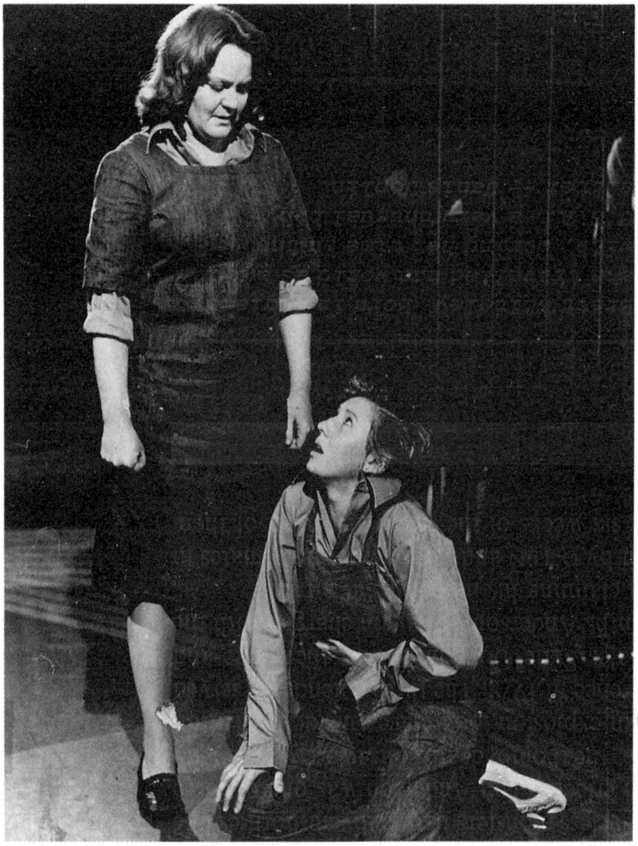

Down, but not out! Frankie Doyle (Carol Burns) tells Bea Smith (Val Lehman) she's top tog 'for now ... but you ain't seen the last or worst of me.' And she's right...

Pate has a shrewd eye for talent. He used Mel Gibson in his pre-cult days for the film of Colleen *'The Thorn Birds'* McCullough's *Tim* (1978).

On location for *The Mango Tree* in Bundaberg, Queensland, Pate said of Carol: 'The lady has tenacity, commitment and a strong desire to succeed. She gets right into the character, and quickly. She'll get something big on television real soon, and there'll be no stopping her.'

When called in by Kerry Spence and Reg Watson to discuss the Doyle role, Burns went straight to the point. 'Great role, folks. But she's a dog, too nasty, too evil. I can see the hate mail pouring in already. Now, justify her behaviour, pull her back a little, and I'll do it.' Watson assured her that that was already done and provided several advance scripts which provided some key insights into Franky's background. It was a big day for Watson when he knew he had Franky Doyle sitting next to him. Franky was based on a real person, 'but I toned her down for the show. The original would have been too shocking'.

Many actresses fought tooth and nail for the part of dual-killer Bea Smith. Agents knew this would be a sensational dramatic role for the right player and the word was out that Bea Smith would be the nemesis of Franky Doyle, if such a thing was possible.

In the end, when the choice was made from the four finalists (no one's telling, but the three who missed out on Bea were to make it to Wentworth later as main players or special guests), none would argue against Grundy's having done it again.

They signed Val Lehman, a stocky, volatile player, mother of two in real life, with considerable experience in theatre and TV – a familiar face but not a name. Playing Queen Bea would change all that overnight. Lehman thrust her poundage and physical strength into Bea like a concrete pile-driver under expert control. Her many confrontations with the formidable Franky Doyle, and later warder Joan Ferguson and all the bashers, killers, druggies and standover merchants that would follow were to give 'Prisoner' some of its most frightening and memorable moments for more than four years and 400 episodes.

Bosom buddies, sharing the ups and downs of Lizzie's troubled times, Val Lehman and Sheila Florance portrayed two of the most enduring characters in Australian TV — the bustling top dog Bea Smith and the eccentric chain-smoker Lizzie Birdsworth

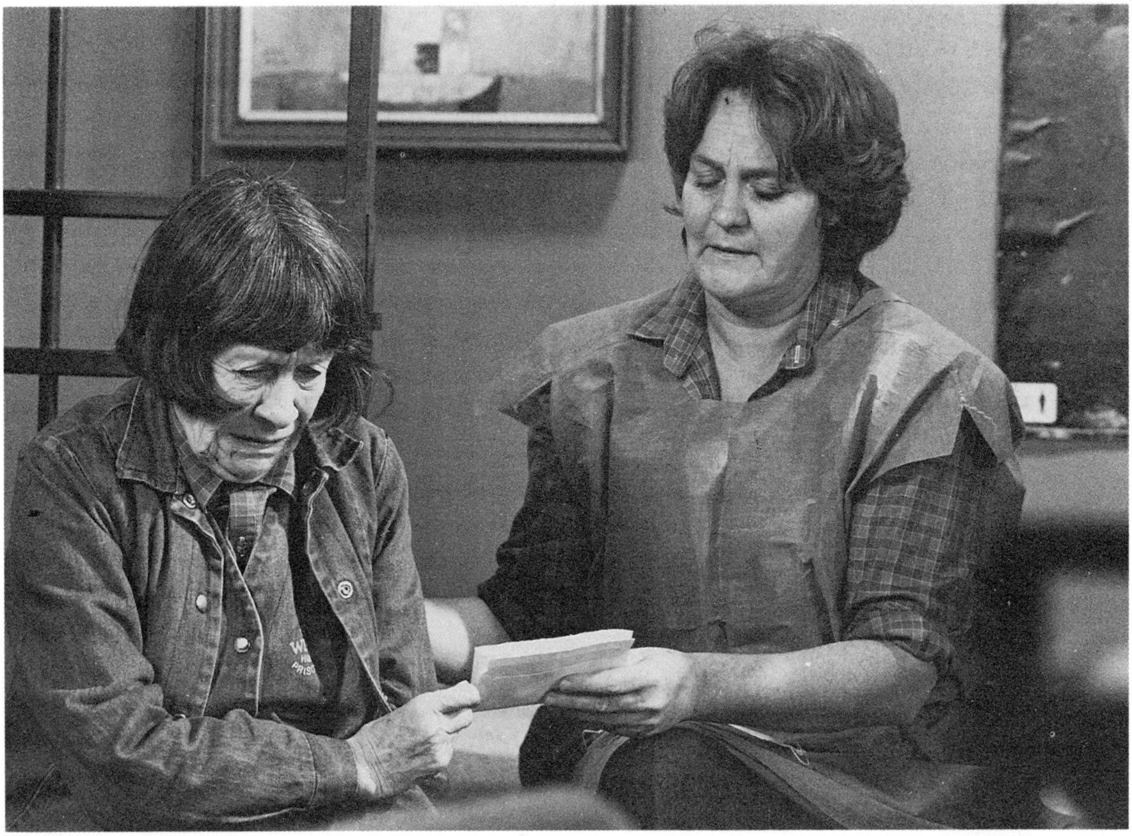

Bea had killed twice. The first time around she murdered a co-worker caught trafficking drugs. Ten years behind bars seemed to mellow the lady, but she didn't like what she saw soon after getting out – her randy husband had taken in another bedmate. And he was part of the chain that supplied drugs to their daughter, who would later die of an overdose despite Bea's vigilance and devotion. So, Bea got hold of a gun and shot him. For this, she got life in Wentworth. Now, no man or woman, including Doyle, will tell her what to do. The constant promise of a fatal showdown between Bea and Franky would be an early strength of 'Prisoner'.

Val, 36 when she signed in at Wentworth, was born in Perth, Western Australia, city of millionaires and once home to the America's Cup. Val chuckles when recalling the highlight of her acting career prior to 'Prisoner'. 'I played a woman in "Bellbird". I was having a baby in the back seat of a Volkswagen. I kid you not.'

When news leaked in Melbourne that Elspeth Ballantyne would play a key role as warder Meg Morris, the press couldn't be kept at bay. The engaging blonde actress, one of Australian television's earliest soap darlings as the winsome Lori Grey in the long-running 'Bellbird' (1963-72), had captured the hearts of viewers not only with her poignant portrayals on screen, but with a real-life, front-page romance and 1968 marriage to 'Bellbird' co-actor Dennis Miller (who played the town cop Des Davies). It was the stuff the best soaps are made of – an at-work romance which led to off-screen wedding bells.

Adelaide-born Elspeth, daughter of actor-playwright Colin Ballantyne (the former boss of the South Australian Theatre Company) and sister of well-known film producer Jane Ballantyne *(Man Of Flowers, My First Wife)*, started her working life cutting up rats in the Royal Adelaide Hospital. 'I was a laboratory technician, and loved it,' she adds. But she caught the acting bug and was in the first intake of students for NIDA (National Institute of Dramatic Art) in 1959. NIDA is Australia's most revered training ground for actors and actresses (Judy Davis and Helen Morse are two of their celebrated graduates).

After graduating, Elspeth worked in many stage productions in Perth, Adelaide and Melbourne before getting the 'Bellbird' role and parts in two movies *End Play* (1975) and *Blue Fin* (1978).

The Meg Morris role in 'Prisoner' would allow Elspeth to play someone her own age (39). Although Meg had a fairly firm grip on life there was plenty of turmoil ahead. She hadn't got seniority stripes for Wentworth the easy way. Her life was turned upside town with the killing of her social worker husband in a prison riot. Her teenage son can't handle the death of his dad and undergoes a remarkable personality change. So, likeable Meg has her family problems.

For the important role of Erica Davidson, Governor of Wentworth, the producers signed Patsy King, who had trained as a Shakespearean actress at the National Theatre in Melbourne. She had guested in many TV shows and was in demand for TV commercial voice-overs. Erica is an authoritative, well-coiffured lady with an open mind about how to run a prison, but she often finds herself quarrelling with ignorant or stubborn jail authorities.

'Erica felt she was running the show as a pretty tight ship, and she generally made sure things were on an even keel. She sought new ways to administer jail routines, and usually attracted loyalty from her staff,' said Patsy. 'I wanted the writers to make her a little more aggro, make her more in absolute control. She wasn't weak, though. I kept telling them she should be more of a heavy, nastier, making enemies which could cost dearly. I suppose they met me halfway by the time I took the final roll-call at Wentworth.'

Second-in-charge at Wentworth was the sadistic warder Vera Bennett, described in the character breakdown for casting as 'the head screw (inmates' nickname for a warder) who rules the prisoners with a hand of steel and an acid, vinegary tongue which snaps commands like a whipcrack'.

It took only a few confrontations between Bea and tough Vera for the inmates and viewers alike to call her Vinegar Tits. The name was bandied around cell-blocks and taken up by thousands of schoolchildren who immediately transferred it to unpopular teachers.

Again Grundy's found the perfect player for 'Beat-em-to-a-pulp Vera' in Fiona Spence. Born in Somerset, England, she was only a baby when her father, a scientist-metallurgist, moved the family to Hong Kong. She later travelled on to Australia and became a schoolgirl thespian. She took a three-year acting course at the New South Wales School of Drama in Sydney. Just before she got the Vera Bennett role, Fiona had shown promise in a small part in the Grundy family series 'Glenview High'.

'I welcomed the chance to play Vera,' recalls Fiona. 'People love to have someone to hate, so I knew Vera would give them all that and more. And it was my first big chance to show my wares. It was quite exciting. I liked the way Vera always schemed, and how badly she wanted to be number one, Governor of Wentworth. The prisoners had their top dog throne, but poor Vera was a constant bridesmaid.'

PRISONER FILE

Name: Margot Gaffney
Actress: Jane Clifton

Armed robber Margot Gaffney was a standover merchant who could ignite explosive riots and organise prisoner resistance. Her chilling reign as top dog ended when the authorities moved her to Blackmore Prison, where they hoped the strict authority and tougher conditions could control her. She was to make return visits, though, as fitted into actress Jane Clifton's busy schedule as a singer-actress.

Peta Toppano (originally Peita, but changed to Peta when she became Australia's undisputed screen goddess in *Return to Eden* and *Fields of Fire III*) was one of the first prisoners. She portrayed the beautiful, victimised Karen Travers, a schoolteacher who kills her husband when she discovers him in bed with another woman after he has forced her to have an abortion. To add to her troubles, the despicable Franky Doyle took an immediate fancy to Karen, whispering such delicacies as, 'We're going to be here night after night, for years and years and years.'

True love would finally rescue Karen from her hell-hole and Franky would transfer her affections elsewhere. But Karen had to contend with months of humiliation, abuse and prolonged court-hearings while her lawyer and lover-doctor organised a retrial and ultimate freedom.

Margaret Laurence, who had attracted plenty of attention as the over-sexed, unfaithful wife of delicatessen manager Arnold Feather (played by Jeff Kevin) in 'Number 96', learned her acting craft in England and America and was the perfect choice for nymphomaniac prisoner Marilyn Mason who, to no one's great surprise, was locked up for prostitution offences. Marilyn and the Wentworth electrician Eddie Cook (played by Richard Moir) made good use of a comfortable cubby-hole near the recreation room and provided the show's few early voyeuristic moments as they unleashed their sexual passions.

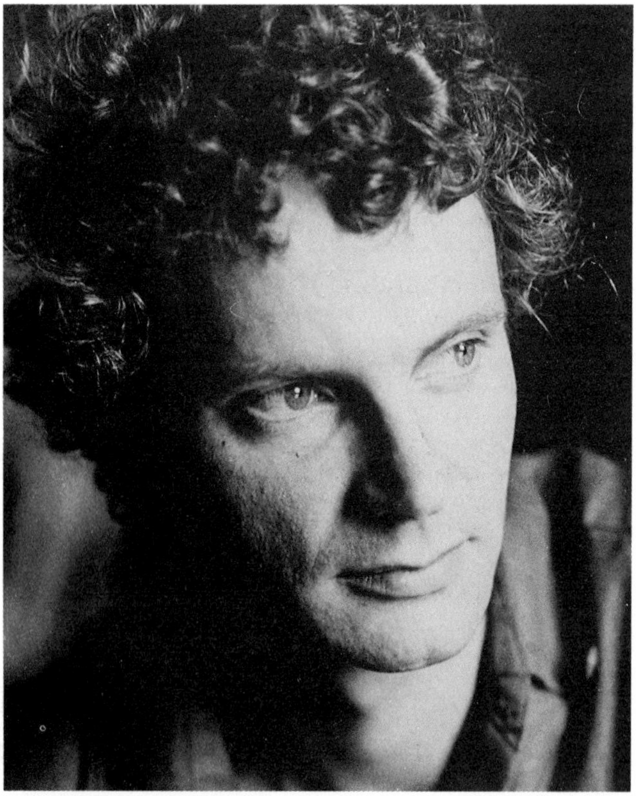

Richard Moir, as electrician Eddie Ward, was among the first of many token males in the show. He and nymphette Marilyn Mason made love in a secret cubby-hole

'Marilyn was the poor man's girly-girly, I suppose,' Margaret says a decade later. 'She was a likeable soul, trying to be good, but she just couldn't. She did what she did best, but could never find true lasting love, not even with Eddie, who adored her. She got out of Wentworth and set up home with him. It still didn't work. It was a case of a girl who couldn't help herself. I grew attached to Marilyn because of the fun side of her, the writers gave me a chance to do things to show her in a better light at times. But in the end it was futile because Marilyn had set herself certain goals which she couldn't possibly reach, and even Eddie's special kind of love couldn't give her those things.'

Doreen Anderson was something of a tubby loner when first introduced to 'Prisoner', child-like and immature for a 19-year-old convict, prone to sucking her thumb and cuddling a teddy-bear at night, she was in the nick for forgery, duped by a so-called boyfriend, yet had lesbian tendencies which made her an obvious target for randy Franky Doyle after she'd been rejected by Karen Travers. Doreen found it hard to make friends, even in the confines of a prison. Some inmates were convinced she was mentally retarded (which she wasn't), and it would take many traumatic events to draw her into the special world of a women's prison.

Colette Mann landed the challenging role of Doreen and she was an early front-runner with fan-mail. Energetic, a former dancer, Colette had done quite a lot of social work and was often an advisor to the scriptwriters.

Monica Ferguson (no relation to the yet-to-be introduced warder Joan 'The Freak' Ferguson), was a basher, a blatant merchant of violence at Wentworth, in and out of jail usually for attacks on her hapless husband, and always scaring the living daylights out of the retinue of floosies he accumulated between Monica's appearances at home.

Muscular, with a broken nose as a legacy of her violent triumph in a brawl over a gang stud, Monica aspired to be top dog, but had Bea Smith and Franky Doyle to contend with, so at the outset she's number three on the power-play list, but it's only too obvious she'll make her move when the time is ripe. Monica adds to her woes early in the series by going into solitary confinement on drug charges.

Grundy's cast against the grain, assigning the Monica role to Lesley Baker, who had been working mainly in comedy roles for twenty years. It was a bold move, and paid off handsomely when Monica quickly developed into a hated and feared barbarian. A bruiser, with ample weight, she would almost pray for Bea or Franky to step in her

PRISONER FILE

Name: Jennifer Bryant

Actress: Susannah Fowle

Silly country girl Jennifer Bryant is missing her mother. So she gets herself sent to jail to join long-term inmate, Judy Bryant by robbing a jewellery store. Obviously, she hasn't heard of visiting hours. . .

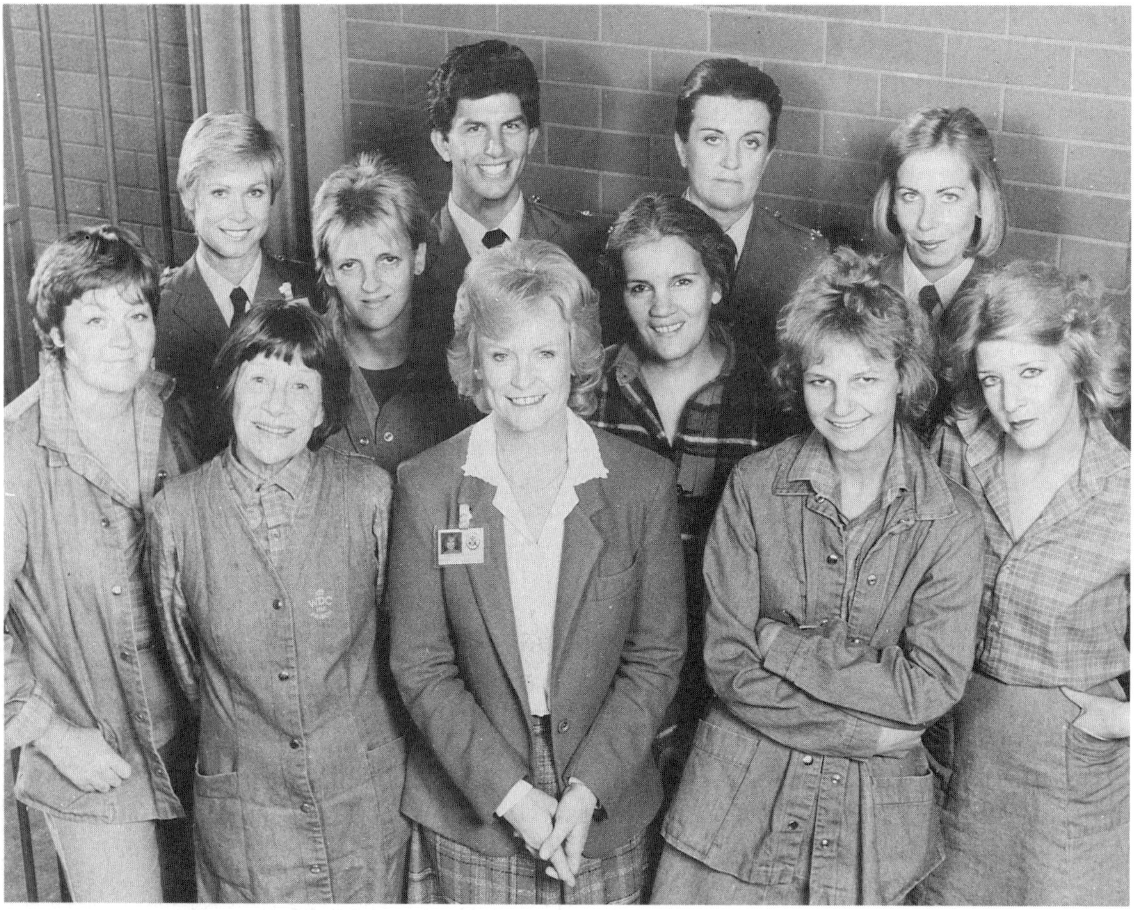

Early-1983 line-up at Wentworth Detention Centre. *Back row*: Meg Morris (Elspeth Ballantyne), Steve Fawkner (Wayne Jarratt), Joan Ferguson (Maggie Kirkpatrick), Colleen Powell (Judith McGrath). *Middle row*: Margot Gaffney (Jane Clifton), Judy Bryant (Betty Bobbitt). *Front row*: Bea Smith (Val Lehman), Lizzie Birdsworth (Sheila Florance), Erica Davidson (Patsy King), Mouse (Jentah Sobott) and Chrissie Latham (Amanda Muggleton)

way. Monica's ongoing problem, other than the fisticuffs and inmate reprisals for her violent ways, was that she spent far too much time in solitary confinement and away from the power base she yearned to rule once Bea and Franky got their comeuppances.

Lesley Baker's earliest claim to fame was as a nightly sidekick, to the comedy players in the top-rating 'In Melbourne Tonight' show, compered by the legendary 'King' Graham Kennedy, who dominated Australian TV for twenty years from its introduction in the mid-Fifties. Today, the King still reigns supreme, with the hilarious oddity, 'Graham Kennedy's Funniest Home Video Show'.

Loads of variety work followed her non-stop IMT years, and Lesley seemed to be in every cop show made at Crawford's (another leading TV production company). 'I started off as a nymphomaniac garage mechanic, then graduated to junior prostitutes and madams and an endless swag of gangsters' wives,' said Lesley.

Kerry Armstrong, later to become a much-publicised guest star in the series 'Dynasty', caused the first sympathy tears at Wentworth. And they turned out to be justified. Kerry was perfect casting as winsome Lynn Warner, a seemingly inoffensive, troubled country girl convicted of kidnapping a baby and trying to bury him alive. It didn't take viewers long to realise Lynn could very well be innocent, and her jealous, psychotic employer the culprit.

Kerry had been in the headlines as a 16-year-old Melbourne schoolgirl who left home in school uniform weekday mornings but at 6.30 each night did a stint 'behind the isobars' as the GTV main news bulletin weather-girl. She spent nearly two weeks making daily visits to Fairlea Prison talking with warders and inmates to get 'proper background feelings' for her stay in Wentworth.

PRISONER FILE

Name: Sandy Edwards

Actress: Louise Le Nay

Sandy Edwards takes over as top dog from Bea Smith for a terror-filled period when Bea is dangerously ill in hospital (in reality when Val Lehman and cast-mates Colette Mann and Gerard Maguire were filming* Kitty and the Bagman*). Edwards is played by NIDA graduate Louise Le Nay who got a shock on her first day at work -- her doctor rang to say she was pregnant. There were considerable disguises used to hide the murderess's bulge until Louise left, seven months pregnant, to have her daughter Victoria.

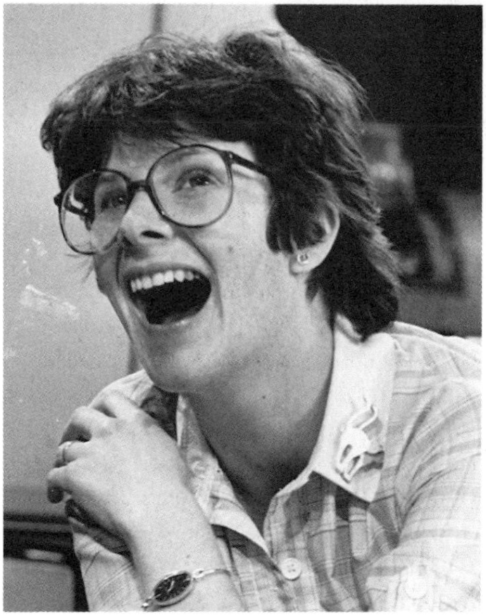

Solo

There was a quaint old lady called Mum Brooks, who had served fifteen years and, expecting to die in jail, made special plans for what little time she thought she had left, concentrating her energies on the small garden the prisoners cultivated outside the main building. This tiny area of hallowed turf gradually became a symbol for Mum and other inmates over the years, despite its limited size and the closeness of a confining 15-foot security fence.

Veteran Mary Ward played institutionalised Mum Brooks, a classic case of how a long-term inmate comes to depend almost entirely on the prison environment to survive and exist. True for many-real-life long-serving prisoners, the show examined this contagious facet of jail life, 'under lock and key dependence', several times, especially with Mum Brooks, and certainly Lizzie Birdsworth. Both these women would commit deliberate petty crimes after their initial release just to get back into prison with their mates. On the outside there was no place for them. Wentworth had become home.

Mum Brooks had been given eighteen years after a headlined euthanasia trial and knew she'd do full time or extra penance. There was no family waiting on the outside to look after her in the twilight years. 'She was a strange old creature in many ways, but wouldn't harm a soul,' said Mary at the time. 'It was amazing how many different people told me Mum reminded them so much of their own mother, aunt or grandmother. People warmed to Mum.'

Mary Ward was born in the bustling port of Fremantle, near Perth, Western Australia, the daughter of a pearler. She remembers vividly fleets of luggers which put out to sea, combing the Indian Ocean for more than 1,400 miles along the west coast, beyond Broome, the pearling capital of the world. 'I was only a young girl, of course. The whole port would turn out to watch the fleet leave – it was much like those rollicking South Pacific adventure films of the Forties and Fifties, with John Wayne or Burt Lancaster but without Dorothy Lamour or Rita Hayworth. Of course, my Dad was my hero.'

Mary began acting professionally soon after leaving school and studying at a Perth drama school. She worked for several years in the U.K. before returning home as one of the first female announcers to be heard regularly on ABC national radio. Widespread TV credits followed more than twenty major stage roles, including 'Skyways', 'Cop Shop', 'Homicide', 'Young Doctors', 'Rush', 'Bellbird', 'Power Without Glory', 'Starting Out' and 'I Can Jump Puddles'.

Amanda Muggleton used a little subterfuge to get into the first few episodes of 'Prisoner', leaving to meet advance stageplay commitments and then returning to Wentworth again under open invitation from the delighted producers and writers, who found a tough, durable, central character in her Chrissie Latham role. And the London-born beauty was a favourite with cast and crew. She had bluffed her way unsuccessfully into the original 'Prisoner' auditions, only to be called back a week later and given the Chrissie part.

Thirty-two-year-old Amanda had strong stage qualifications. A graduate of the

Guild Hall School of Music and Drama (London), she was a winner of the prestigious City of London Festival Players Award, and came to Australia in 1974 as a member of the English Theatre Company. When the tour ended she decided to stay on, first in Sydney, then moving south, where she became a stalwart with the Melbourne Theatre Company. So began the first of many *Steaming* performances – wherever the play opened in Australia, it seemed Amanda was there strutting her stuff with a brief towel as her only covering. By the time the gates finally closed at Wentworth, Chrissie Latham had been in and out five times. During that tenure she had killed the husband of a female warder, had a baby, and generally proved indestructible.

Amanda recalls that early 'Prisoner' casting session. 'My agency hadn't chased any of the roles for me because I had advance contracts for *Steaming*, but when I heard about a call for a women's prison show at Grundy's I sneaked in to the audition rooms. This young assistant with a clipboard said, "You're not listed for today, so I can't fit you in". Well, I got a little stroppy and told her firmly I'd been asked to be there at 4 p.m. and I'd travelled a long way to be there, and within minutes they were auditioning me. But I missed out. I thought that's the end of that, I'm not going to prison. Days later they advised my agent it had been decided I was better suited for the Chrissie Latham role. It took them another agonising four days to call again and confirm I had the job.

Chrissie Latham's background was that of a petty criminal who grew bolder and more ambitious, moving on to major crime and armed robbery. 'She's a real schemer, shyster supreme and cunning player of mind and body games,' said Amanda at the time she signed for the series. 'It's fun playing her – and I can get out every now and then to do a play or a TV show, so I'm not really locked up, am I?'

Other than Eddie Cook's electrifying pursuits of the always willing and obliging nymphette Marilyn Mason, the token male line-up in the initial episodes of 'Prisoner' was limited to prison doctor Greg Miller (Barry Quin, who later in real life would marry actress Peta Toppano, the lady playing his love interest in the series), jail psychiatrist Bill Jackson (Adelaide actor Don Barker), occasional lawyers, medical and staff cohorts. But the male strength would be increased and make a big impact on Wentworth's near all-woman world once the series was up and running.

The major roles for 'Prisoner' had been assigned, contracts drawn up and a shooting schedule readied. Rounding off a unique assembly of actresses playing the inmates was the first actress to be considered for the jail drama. She was a remarkable veteran with an astonishing true-life story that a Hollywood script-writer would be hard pressed to imagine. She was to make Lizzie Birdsworth, Wentworth's 'old chook', a household name around the world.

4

LIZZIE: DEAD MEN DO TELL TALES

What Sheila Florance first thought of lesbian Franky and her tattoos is anyone's guess. But she read the early scripts with relish ('even glee', she would reveal later) and had no hesitation in taking the role of frail, weather-beaten ('I've seen life and life's seen me') cigarette-addicted, Lizzie Birdsworth.

You would have thought Sheila had had enough of bikies. Only four months earlier she had broken a knee filming a tricky, somewhat dangerous action scene at a country farmhouse for Mel Gibson's *Mad Max* movie. Brandishing a lethal double-barrelled shotgun, Sheila was chasing a rampaging bikie when she trod in a hole and fell heavily. Several days later, leg and hip in plaster, this marvellous old lady (she was then 62) hobbled back to work to finish her two uncompleted scenes.

Director George Miller and cameraman David Eggby made sure they didn't film her below the waist. 'At my age, darling, I should have known better – clutching a loaded shotgun, running after bikies. Oh, it did hurt when I fell, believe me. But I was more concerned about the antique shotgun I was carrying. It was priceless, one of a kind, hired at some outrageous fee from a nervous collector, worth $18,000 (£8,650). Special effects and props had continuously warned me their necks were on the chopping block if anything happened to the rifle.

'Well, they made sure the gun was OK before director George arrived to take charge – he was a real-life doctor and, until a few weeks before *Mad Max* started shooting, had been working shifts in casualty hospitals to help finance the film. George felt around my swollen knee and assured me, "Lucky girl, no break." As a doctor, George is a great director. Luckily, the ambulance officers knew straightaway I had broken the knee, and they sort of settled me down before zipping me off to hospital and surgery.'

Mel Gibson called Sheila 'a hell of a dame – bloody great trouper – a few days after being carted off in an ambulance she's back on set on crutches with this gigantic plaster cast and asking, "What do you want me to do now?" If George (Miller) had said, "Climb Mount Everest", I'm sure Sheila would have said, "Now, or after breakfast?" What a lady!'

This brave show of loyalty and commitment to her work and mates typifies much of what has amazed people about the life and times of Sheila Florance. Her bad times would have stopped the faint-hearted in their tracks, if not put them out for the count.

Sheila was only 18 and an aspiring stage actress when she met visiting English law student Roger Oyston in Melbourne. They married after a short whirlwind romance. 'In those days you just didn't marry that young – we're talking about the Thirties. Convention had it you were required to court and have a long and meaningful engagement,' says Sheila, smiling between quick draws on her cigarette. 'And me, a former boarder at Presentation Convent, Melbourne.

'My dad was a bonzer bloke, though', says Sheila. 'He was totally supportive of the marriage, bless him. A schoolteacher, years ahead of his time, a tremendously intellectual man who taught at Caulfield Grammar. I'm fourth generation Australian, a volatile mixture of Italian, Irish and Scots ancestry. Mother was one of the first women to qualify as a dentist in Melbourne. She was a great wit, but strict, and used to thump me if I spoke ocker. She was the niece of Peter Lalor, who led the miners' rebellion at the Eureka Stockade in 1854 – her dad was John Lalor, Peter's younger brother. Any rate it was Dad who encouraged me into the theatre as a young girl. I wanted to do Shakespeare exclusively, and did, for a long time. I never thought I'd end up doing old

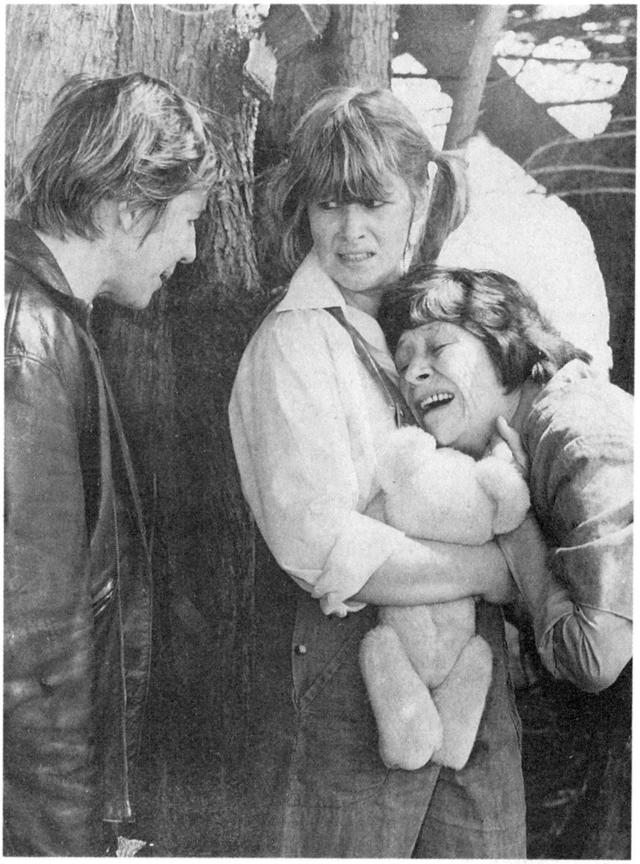

'Leave the old lag, otherwise we'll be caught trying to cart her along,' says Franky Doyle (Carol Burns) after Lizzie Birdsworth (Sheila Florance) contracts chest pains during an escape bid. However, Doreen Campbell (Colette Mann) doesn't want to leave Lizzie behind ... but they do, and tragedy ensues

ocker Lizzie in jail but Dad wouldn't have minded. He was my toughest critic and my best tutor. I might have been a surgeon or a doctor if he hadn't pushed me on stage, and if I'd been a fella, well, I'd have been a sailor.

'I was only a slip of a girl when I met Roger. We were wonderfully in love within days of our first meeting. Why? Who knows? Yes, he swept me off my feet. And I must have done the same to him. I decided I'd rather have some babies than do more plays. Roger wanted to take me home to England to meet his folks. So, with five-month-old baby Peter in my arms we sailed to the U.K. – all very strange for a 19-year-old mother in those days.

'If I had known what was going to happen to Roger and our baby daughter I would never have gone over there or stayed so long – but we were happy. Both Roger and I were working, and our family grew to two boys and a girl. The famous British actress Ada Reeves "discovered" me at the Little Theatre and insisted I try bigger roles. Soon after, I landed a major role in a West End play called *Mother of Pearl.* I was getting seven pounds a week. Later I'd work with Emlyn Williams, Noel Coward, Robert Donat and Dame Sybil Thorndike. Everything was coming up roses.'

The outbreak of war changed all that, and Sheila was about to endure 'the worst years of my life'. Roger Oyston went missing after the Normandy landings in 1944. It took the War Ministry almost a year to advise finally he had been killed in action, although Sheila had resigned herself to the horrible truth days after they reported him missing.

'I managed to get regular stage work during those dreadful times. I was on my way to join the Bristol Old Vic, and had just stepped off the train at Templemeads Station with my 10-month-old baby daughter in my arms when they sounded the air-raid siren which meant you stayed underground or headed for the nearest shelter. I was petrified, amid all the panic.'

Sheila finds it hard to go on. Even forty-five years later memories are all too vivid. The bombing had started. The sirens drowned out the drone of the German bomber squadrons high in the sky. Buildings two platforms away and the roofs above them were exploding in flames, causing giant swirls of dust, and through that came cascading steel, burning wood and concrete slabs. Then, like shadowy ghosts, scores of people reeled out of the smoke, holding bloodied heads, or helping others to safety.

'They were yelling and screaming. A bomb dropped near me and my baby was blown from my arms and killed. It happened so quickly. I was on my knees amid the rubble, choking in dust and smoke. I could see a few bodies and injured passengers. But there was no sign of my baby.'

Sheila doesn't like dwelling on the past, and rarely talks of the war tragedies and subsequent struggle to survive. 'I lost so many dear friends in the London blitz and the losses of Roger and the baby were dreadful. Luckily, I was working with all these wonderful people – the women were amazing. Some of us had lost husbands or sons, everyone had lost someone. There were all those fine boys and men, too, forced to forsake what may have been great careers on the stage. They went off to fight the war and never came back. A sad, savage waste.'

It was some consolation for Sheila that she could work with entertainment groups performing for Allied troops, which was when she had the pleasure of working with Noel Coward. 'We all felt we were doing something for the boys. A distinct purpose in life.'

At the end of the war, Sheila met a handsome Polish pilot by the name of John Balawaider, flying with the RAF Bomber Command. 'I should have been in the Polish Squadron, but was drafted into the British Air Force by mistake,' John said in a rare interview soon after Sheila became a national star in 'Prisoner'. 'I flew Halifax bombers over France and Germany for more than half the war. My crew was made up of five Englishmen, with a young man from Sydney as wireless operator.'

During a raid over Germany on 2 February 1945 John's Halifax was hit several times by ground fire, and three large pieces of flak were embedded in his legs. How he managed to get the battered bomber back to base remains a mystery. His squadron commander inspected the Halifax and John the following morning as John lay in hospital awaiting the first of several operations that would remove most of the metal fragments, although he would never regain normal use of his legs. 'Absolute miracle either of you got back. Magnificent flying, John,' said the commander. Seventeen days

PRISONER FILE

Name: Chrissie Latham

Actress: Amanda Muggleton

Abrasive, menacing Chrissie Latham was in and out of Wentworth all the time. Every time she left, there were hundreds of viewers' letters asking when she was to return to antagonise Bea and the warders. Said actress Amanda Muggleton, 'Playing Chrissie is a piece of cake, despite the brutality and venom which often surround her. I can come and go as I please, too, so I'm not really locked up, am I?'

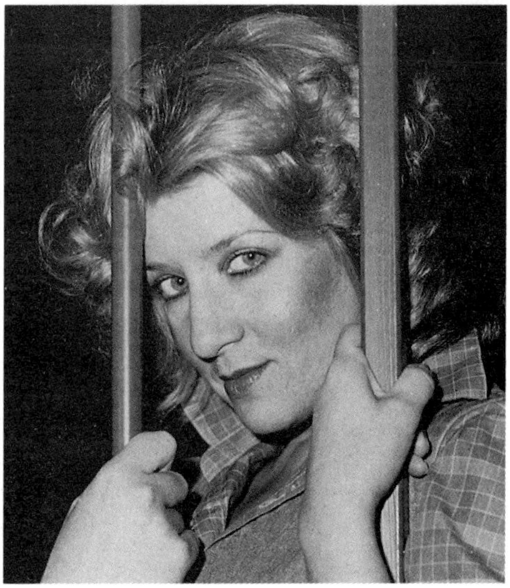

later a nurse brought a message to him. His Halifax crew had been shot down over Germany. 'All had died,' John says softly.

After the war, when John was able to get around under his own steam, he and Sheila 'hit it off very well' and when they married in Nottingham Cathedral, a full Polish choir was in attendance. 'Beautiful, just beautiful,' says Sheila, eyes moist, her words fading as she remembers those celebratory voices of forty-four years ago.

But trouble lay ahead for the newly-weds. 'Although stateless, John had an exit permit because he was in the services,' explains Sheila. 'I had acquired Polish nationality because of my new marriage and wasn't eligible to return to Australia. Red tape and bureaucracy in those days of readjustment was incredibly laborious, and for many families like John and myself and the kids, so painful. I was in England with a new husband and two sons, one of them born in Australia and I was an alien, without a country. I was supposed to go to a country behind the Iron Curtain. Truly, that's what they wanted me to do.'

Of course, Sheila wouldn't take any of this lying down, and did 'a blackmail job' on the staff at Australia House in London. She went on a sit-down hunger strike outside their main offices and, not wanting an international incident, the bureaucrats gave in.

More trouble! The British Foreign Office had confiscated Sheila's passport, and she had to apply for a new one and spend weeks waiting for it to be authorised and made available. And that made it hard to book their passage home.

The newly-weds were separated for a few months. John was able to fly out to Australia because of his war credentials, but Sheila and the two boys spent several months in an overcrowded passenger ship carrying war refugees from London to Melbourne.

PRISONER FILE

Name: Kay White

Actress: Sandy Gore

Middle-class, well educated Kay White is the Girl Friday in a clothing factory, super-organised and the boss's right hand. Unfortunately, her right hand is in the till and she's a compulsive gambler.

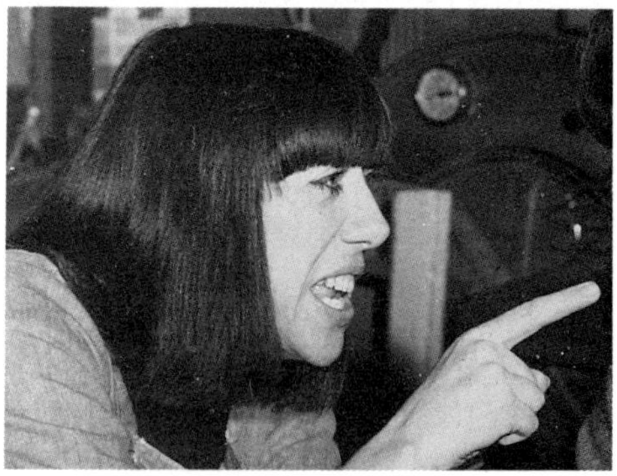

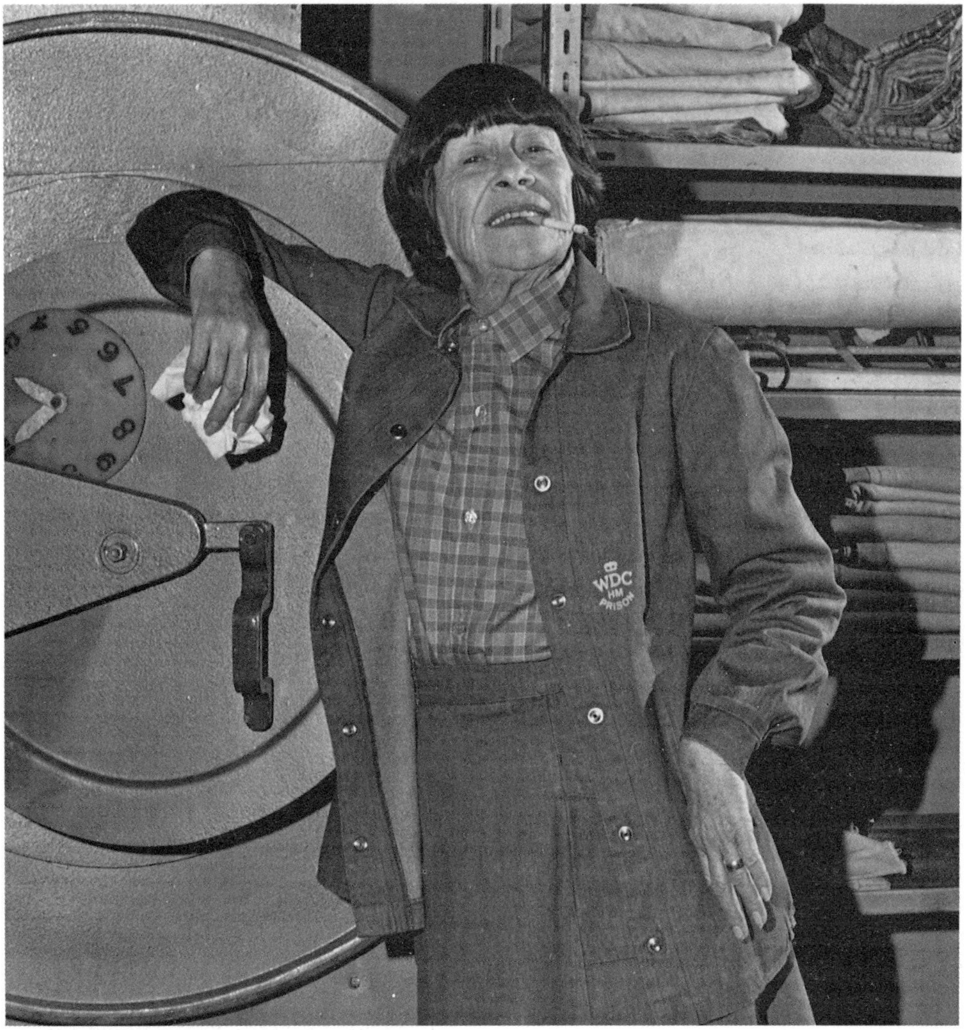

'Now this is what I call high glam,' says Lizzie Birdsworth (Sheila Florance) after being outfitted in new Wentworth gear in late 1984. *(Solo Syndication)*

'Once down the gangway and through customs, I hot-footed it straight to St. Kilda like a homing pigeon,' says Sheila. 'Heavens, what an absolute joy to be home again, to see the old place for the first time in sixteen years. Old faces along the street, even the trees and shrubs. Of course, lovely, smiling John was there to make it all so perfect.'

John's niggling war injuries got worse and more painful and he became an invalid. Sheila was his devoted mate and nurse, but John insisted Sheila get out and enjoy herself away from family life. He could at least keep an eye on the growing boys when they were not at school. Sheila went back into acting, winning numerous awards with the famous J. C. Williamson Theatre Company and top touring companies. But she was still very preoccupied with the boys and caring for John, and choosey about what shows she signed for. A week or two away from her beloved John and St. Kilda was as much as she could stand.

Her peers and colleagues knew Sheila as one of the most experienced actresses in the land and possessed of indefatigable energy. Thin, slimly built, but tough when she wanted to be, Sheila had played an array of old ladies in the likes of 'Bellbird' and all the Crawford cop shows. 'I wore these different hats playing five old dears in "Bellbird", and no one could remember my face – the hats, yes, they'd remember the hats.'

Then, in 1977, a TV producer from Sydney, Reg Watson, contacted her and said he was doing a series called 'Women Behind Bars', and there was this part of an old lag. Of Lizzie Birdsworth, Watson told Sheila: 'She sort of hangs around in the background, faking a heart-attack or two now and then. And, oh yes, you'll have to take your teeth out on camera. Are you interested?'

Lizzie Birdsworth was a cigarette-puffing arthritic lady 'with a head of sawdust and heart of gold'. In Wentworth for life, she'd poisoned four sheep shearers who were boarding at her place. They had had the audacity to complain about her cooking. So for good measure Lizzie gave them a huge dose of arsenic. Lizzie subscribed to the credo 'Dead men tell no tales'. However, forensic science does . . .

Sheila was the only main player in the original Wentworth cast not required to read or audition. Yes, she did have to agree to taking out her teeth. 'Nothing hard or silly about that, my love,' says Sheila.

Reg Watson will tell you he saw a photograph of Sheila, and was astounded when he read her endless list of credits over nearly fifty years of acting. He immediately made contact with her to talk about playing old Lizzie.

Sheila continues: 'She sounded like a fascinating lady. I think I fell in love with her the first time I read the scripts. I remember thinking there was a lot you could add or work into Lizzie. She seemed to be a dear old soul, but capable of being a bit of a nuisance without really knowing it and she'll do anything to get her own way. Yet she's incredibly maternal. She tries to protect all the defenceless ones.

'I guess in the end, I was being asked to play myself, give or take a few of Lizzie's edges and quirks. Any rate, in these days of young people's shows and all the glossy American soaps, producers usually don't chase actresses my age with offers. How could I refuse?'

5

THE FINAL COUNTDOWN

The 'Prisoner' casting offices in Sydney and Melbourne had been working overtime for the past month, after an initial two months of talent-spotting and auditions. Now, in several workshops at the Channel O studios, the art department, wardrobe and props team were doing their share.

Art director Ian Costello utilised more than 350 reference photographs and sketches of Melbourne and Sydney prison exteriors and interiors to build a series of special sets which ranged from claustrophobic cells and corridors to the Wentworth Detention Centre laundry, the recreation room and library. There were sets for the adminstration area, including reception, the governor's office, staff quarters, hospital and a truck bay. And, of course, that passion pit of a cubbyhole into which Marilyn Mason and Eddie Cook crawled.

While the writers played close attention to official protocol requirements, prison slang, nicknames and real-life stories, the enterprising designers, props folk and set dressers went to extraordinary lengths to be totally realistic about the look and feel of the prison sets. Lockers had prisoners' names on them, and now, the final names were being added daily as the Australia-wide casting campaign drew to an end.

Set dresser Geoff Hatton contracted a private printing firm to provide the official Wentworth Detention Centre seal, insignia and appropriate stationery, highlighted by the official jail letterhead which would pass even the closest camera scrutiny over the ensuing seven years.

The sets were ready at Channel O (later to be absorbed into the O-TEN Network of international media magnate Rupert Murdoch). The back of the studio building served as the entrance gate and main wall of Wentworth, and the station's massive transmitting tower was camouflaged as the jail watchtower, complete with patrol guards, dominating the Wentworth skyline day and night.

Shooting on Episode One of 'Prisoner' was scheduled to begin on Wednesday, 4 August 1978, after two days of rehearsals and blocking camera moves for location and studio sequences. A sprinkling of extra background prisoners from the Melbourne casting offices was chosen that morning, although the uniformed extras wouldn't be needed for the initial scenes.

In the studio the massive overhead lighting grid was getting a final check by a team of technicians. Director of photography 'Swifty' Swift knew he would be taping the biggest show put together at Channel O. He was happy to have Burt Smith, of London Weekend TV, to help advise on lighting and camerawork. Smith is regarded as one of U.K.'s best lighting men, well versed in capturing the images of shows like 'Prisoner'. 'Don't make the mistake of making it look too drab,' he had told Reg Watson.

By 8.10 a.m. it would have been all systems go in the studio – but 'Prisoner's' first shots were being taped fifteen miles across town without any sign of a prison uniform. Viewers wouldn't see this footage until Episode Nine, when the dramatic and shocking truth about Lynn Warner would be vividly revealed.

'Prisoner' was finally before the cameras. It was 397 days since Ian Holmes had given Reg Watson the go-ahead.

The first scene shot for 'Prisoner' called for a palatial mansion in the exclusive suburb of Toorak, home to many of Melbourne's richest and most influential families. Over the opening shot of the sprawling, luxury home and its landscaped gardens could be heard the frantic, pleading cries of a young woman.

Lynn Warner (with Kerry Armstrong screaming her head off for the first two hours of the Toorak shoot) was being sexually assaulted and abused by a man (well-known Melbourne actor Frank Gallacher), the screen husband of the schizophrenic socialite Marlene Beecher (actress Arianthe Galani). It was Madame Beecher who would fabricate the bizarre tale of her infant baby's abduction and burial alive.

Director Graeme Arthur recalled everyone 'being on some sort of an edge' that first morning. A few days later, he told a reporter, 'We'd planned, rehearsed the action and dialogue. Everyone knew what was expected of them, and what was happening storywise – yet there was this mixture of apprehension, over-hype and aggressive energy. Once we got the house shots and Kerry's big scenes, everything fell into place and it was like we'd been doing the show for weeks, not a few hours.'

Naive, winsome Lynn was a perfect stooge for callous, conniving Marlene Beecher. A lonely country girl, in the big smoke for the first time without family or friends. Then a seemingly wonderful, elegant, rich lady offered her a baby-sitting job. It had to be a godsend. Little did Lynn know she was being dragged down a nightmare path, leading to Wentworth Jail.

'Prisoner' had two full-time directors when it launched – Graeme Arthur and Rod Hardy. Reg Watson wrote the first episode, and Episodes Two and Five; producer Ian Bradley penned Episodes Three, Four and Nine; while Denise Morgan and Michael Brindley wrote the remaining ten shows. This finely tuned creative team worked around a complicated schedule orchestrated by producers Bradley and Philip East (later to move to 'Neighbours'). Arthur was shooting exteriors and interiors such as the first day at Toorak, while Hardy was in the studio preparing the next episode. Later, additional directors would join the team.

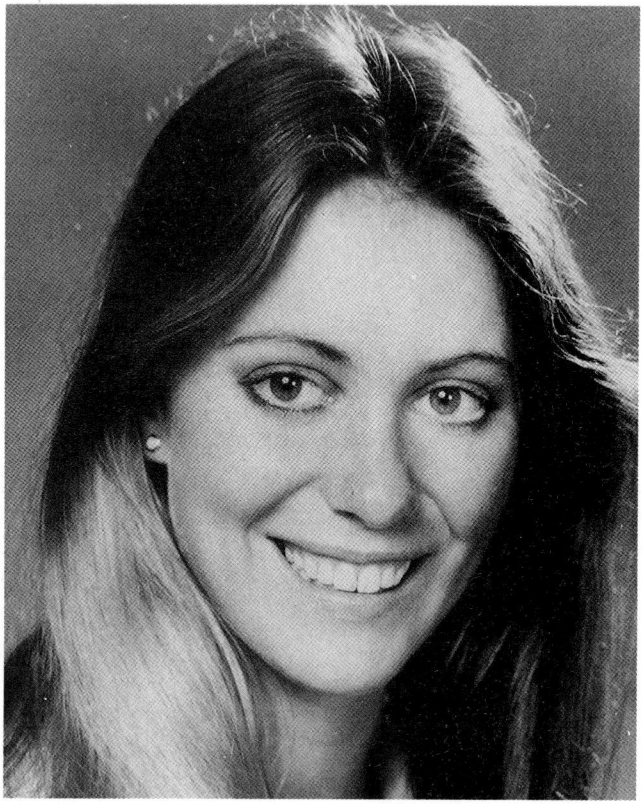

Could this petite country beauty kidnap a baby and try to bury him alive? Lissome Lynn Warner (Kerry Armstrong) protested her innocence ... and she was telling the truth!

One-hour shows for commercial airings are forty-eight minutes long, leaving twelve minutes for commercials and network IDs to be inserted. The first episodes of 'Prisoner' were designed to hook viewers in a matter of minutes, get solid word-of-mouth interest and, of course, impress the media. 'If the show didn't work in the first weeks it wouldn't work at all,' one nervous Grundy producer said as taping got underway. 'We don't have any real nagging doubts about "Prisoner", but with TV shows, you're playing a lottery. Some you win, some you lose.'

At the outset, 'Prisoner' was costing $55,000 (£26,000) a week to produce, but when the schedule moved to two episodes a week the two hours rose beyond $80,000 (£38,000). At the peak of its popularity in 1984 the budget was more than $120,000 (£57,000) per week. By Australian standards that was about average for taped drama, but well below the Crawford Productions hit on Channel Nine, 'The Flying Doctors' ($14O-180,000 or £67,600-86,000 per hour, but shot on the more expensive medium of film).

From day one there was a feeling of 'reality among all us girls. It was actually happening: it wasn't hard to act, to pretend we were in jail,' Mary Ward recalled. 'It made for exciting scenes, especially the fights and confrontations between Franky and Bea.'

The intensity of the acting was unknown in Australian drama. Players threw themselves into their characters. Just how real some of the scenes became was clearly illustrated in the celebrated Franky Doyle library-wrecking sequence. Doyle went on an out-of-control rampage. The fury of Carol Burns up-ending and smashing furniture and books in a frenzy of demolition scared everyone on the set, including Bradley. 'Carol got so involved in the scene she had to be physically calmed down and told the sequence was over. Some lark asked if we were going to do it again? Before the director had a chance to answer, I said, "No way," it just couldn't have been done. It was a scene I'll never forget.'

Burns admits she left the set 'hands trembling, head throbbing, minor muscle pain and vision blurred, and I was sweating like a pig.' Crew members were shaken, and experienced cameramen shook their heads in amazement when the set calmed down.

Burns adds: 'One of the prison extras was this poor girl learning her way around a TV set, a first-timer. At the height of the action she took refuge by hiding under a table, crying her eyes out. She was scared out of her wits and had to be coaxed out. There were some days like that. It was all or nothing with Franky in the more intense scenes.'

Val Lehman and Carol remember the bruises, the cuts to their arms and hands. 'Whenever there was a fight scene or a brawl we had stunt choreographers, of course, but did virtually all the action ourselves. Fingers were the easiest things to hurt. After a few weeks there weren't any more spots for me to get bruises,' says Val. 'We were so much into the roles we went at it hammer and tongs. I got quite a few hefty smacks across the face. Sloppy, sloppy girl,' mused Val.

'Me, too,' says Carol. 'I wasn't the only wild swinger in Wentworth. The crew were amazed at those early fights. They couldn't figure out if we were really hammering each

PRISONER FILE

Name: Hannah Simpson
Actress: Julieanne Newbould

Naive Hannah Simpson is in Wentworth to serve her first sentence for armed robbery. Young and beautiful, she believes she has the right to steal from other people and soon becomes an obvious target for the Freak. Julieanne Newbould said when she signed up for 'Prisoner', 'I'm facing with equanimity the prospect of being seduced by a lesbian prison officer.'

And four years later, Julieanne turns up again, this time as undercover cop, Wendy Glover, trying to get inside information. With a new hair style and different mannerisms, there was little resemblance to Hannah.

other, or if we were pulling punches and doing a great job as stuntwomen. The confined space was usually the main problem.'

Colette Mann and Margaret Laurence were usually spared these agonies, but they were traumatised onlookers. 'We were all into character so quick, but I remember being numb just watching Val and Carol hammer away at each other or whoever was in their way,' said Colette. And Margaret remembers, 'For a few weeks I used to panic when the scripts arrived. I was scared silly thinking my time would come and it would be my turn to get the treatment. Luckily it never happened.'

Sheila Florance says she doesn't remember much about the first weeks of 'Prisoner' shooting, 'save that it was exciting for an old girl like me to be in a TV series, and making friends so quickly. They all gave me a lot of help. I do remember that everyone hit it off fabulously from the first scenes, and I just used to marvel at how strong Val and Carol could be, and me, an old, doddering thing watching them. Of course, I'm no fool. I was learning all the time. Remember, an ongoing TV role was fairly new to me. Val was a great teacher. We became great buddies. Generally, we all were good friends. We had to be, living in each others' pockets for twelve or more hours a day. You can't keep any secrets with a set full of unusual characters and just as unusual players. We were all close, but Val, Colette and Fiona were special to me. It wasn't like mother and daughters, more like a bunch of sisters. I was so happy.'

Weeks after a very poignant scene involving Carol Burns, Sheila's eyes were moist. 'Franky learns of her young brother's death, and she blames herself as she lays on her bunk clutching the little boy's jacket. The tears, real ones, roll down her cheek. I was in the cell next door listening to all this, and I suddenly burst into tears – they weren't scripted. I couldn't control myself and, immediately they cut the cameras, Carol and I ran off the set crying our eyes out. I'll never forget that scene. Carol was magnificent.'

Soon came the first rumours that there wouldn't be a close-down on the series. 'Someone from Grundy's said we were on a goer, that is, the show would go on for a longer period. We had contracts for only sixteen episodes. They had an option on our services beyond that, of course, but at the time we were not really thinking beyond the first batch,' says Sheila.

Tragedy struck the 'Prisoner' gang in the middle of Episode Thirteen. Cast and crew arrived on set one Thursday morning in mid-August to the shattering news that popular regular director Graeme Arthur had died at his Albert Park home overnight of a massive heart-attack. He was only 35. The day before Graeme had seemed happy, fit and in good health.

'I was stunned. It was the blackest day I can remember as far as "Prisoner" was concerned,' said producer Bradley. 'Graeme was like family. He'd been with the show since its advent. It cast a pall of gloom over the studio. But we all knew we had a show to keep on the road.'

The completion of Episodes Fourteen, Fifteen and Sixteen were close at hand, only weeks away. Then there would be the Christmas and New Year holidays. But the O-TEN management were thinking further into the future. Ian Holmes announced O-TEN wanted an additional twenty-six one-hour episodes of 'Prisoner'. 'And that's before a single episode had been shown to the public,' added Holmes. 'It's the best vote of confidence I have ever heard for an Australian drama series.'

The word was out that 'Prisoner' was a sensation, a big hit in the making. This was no publicity hype. Some influential media people had managed to get a peek at the first shows. Rival network executives were having their worst fears confirmed. Grundy's was giving O-TEN a ratings winner of new dimensions. This show could run for years, they were told. Wentworth would soon be the new name on everyone's lips. The commitment to further episodes even before they'd screened an episode was seen as a seal of total approval by the network. And eager advertising agencies with heavyweight national and overseas clients were lining up to get the best commercial spots in 'Prisoner' once the show got underway.

But there was still the general press, and with the subject matter of 'Prisoner' the media jungle was bound to harbour a few snipers. The Australian press had long been accused of promoting the tall poppy syndrome: 'Build 'em up, then chop 'em down.' But the O-TEN and Grundy hierarchy knew sooner or later they'd have to face the media flak, and hoped there would be more praise than damnation.

D-Day neared. The O-TEN Network publicity machine went into action with national publicity director Brian Walsh pulling out all the stops. Walsh knew that by the time the show unveiled he had to guarantee 'Prisoner' was 'known everywhere, in every nook and cranny. My mission is to make sure there isn't a soul in *Terra australis* who won't know about "Prisoner" in the coming weeks.'

Veteran TV industry chronicler Ben Mitchell (*TV Soap*) recalls, 'You'd have had to be blind, deaf, out of the country or on another planet not to have known about "the new, big, daring, bold series". There were even full-page promotional advertisements in

PRISONER FILE

Name: Marie Winter

Actress: Maggie Millar

A chill in her name and ice in her veins -- Marie Winter has a hideous record of crime, specialising in dope. A brawling, cursing, spitting felon, she makes the most of Bea Smith's absence in hospital to seize the top dog throne. She brutalises her foolhardy opponents and the inmates are soon desperate for hard but fair Bea's victorious comeback. The prison authorities recognise Winter's mayhem and send her off to finish her sentence in maximum security at Blackmore Prison.

the major city dailies. It all had the magic touch of Walsh and O-TEN on the road to a ratings bonanza.'

One final acid test for acceptance of 'Prisoner's première episodes was Reg Watson's decision to show the reels to Sandra Willson, a key consultant to the writers, and Australia's longest-serving female prisoner. A convicted murderess, she had spent eighteen years in jail from 1958 to 1976 before being freed after heavy campaigning across Australia by women's action groups.

'I valued Sandra's comments more than anyone else in the weeks leading up to the preview screenings,' recalls Watson. 'Sandra gave us the thumbs-up all the way. You couldn't ask for a better review.'

There was, however, and for no obvious reason, a growing belief in the hard core group of Sydney and Melbourne TV critics that 'Prisoner' 'would probably be another typical package out of the Grundy sausage factory'. But they'd have to wait for the launch to write their verdict in ink. Grundy's O-TEN and the cast and crew were quietly confident they would come up trumps with the media. After that, it would be up to the viewers.

The hard-working Wentworth team at the Melbourne studios of O-TEN were already on Episodes Twenty-one and Twenty-two when the previews were held, and were more concerned about remembering their lines and not bumping into the furniture than the media reactions. But the press wanted to talk to the stars, and several were despatched to run the gauntlet. Prisoner and jailer alike, they all waited for the presses to roll.

Bob Gordon, then editor of the *TV Extra Magazine* in the Australian *Women's Weekly* (the country's biggest-selling magazine, published by media magnate Kerry Packer, soon to be Australia's richest man, and owner, too, of the Nine Network) remembers the 'Prisoner' launch. 'I hadn't seen a foot of "Prisoner" tape, and only a few publicity shots and press-kit info sheets. I had journalists in Melbourne and Sydney covering the show's progress. But I knew by the way O-TEN bosses were carrying on that "Prisoner" would be a winner.

'It's not a matter of having an editorial nose to predict success in soapland. Every now and then an exceptional Australian show comes along – Jimmy Davern had done it with "A Country Practice" for the Seven Network, just as he did eighteen years earlier with "Bellbird" for the ABC, which wrote the book for Aussie soaps. TV pioneer Hector Crawford did it with his Melbourne-based cop shows "Homicide", "Division Four", "Matlock Police", and later, "The Sullivans" and "Cop Shop". Hector had a nose for long runners. And here was "Prisoner" coming on like a storm to belt the opposition. A lot of us felt this was a time for Grundy's, a time for O-TEN.'

And it was.

6

THE AUSTRALIAN VERDICT

So began the first of 'Prisoner' media previews in the two main cities, Sydney and Melbourne – reviewers, feature writers and regular TV journalists were flown in from interstate capital cities of Perth, Adelaide, Canberra, Hobart and Brisbane.

The previews were timed to coincide with the week leading up to the 27 February 1979 premières on Channels O and TEN in Melbourne and Sydney. Brian Walsh, O-TEN publicity boss, remembers 'the waiting. The network had ordered extra episodes without one being tested or seen on air, which in itself was unheard of. So we felt fairly safe and happy – but you can never tell in this business.'

Bob Gordon (*Women's Weekly*) picks up the story. 'Reviewers might have had some doubts over those first episodes. It seemed severe in some aspects, but most of us were smart enough to know something special was there and the viewers would make the decision. If there were any doubts, we did the safe thing and opted for a revisit to Wentworth down the track. But there was no denying it was different, tougher than we'd expected, no punches pulled, and all in a women's world. We had sort of expected it to work, even if we didn't trumpet it at first, and the new faces were a big bonus.'

Don Groves, writing in the Sydney *Sun-Herald* predicted, 'If the standard of the first few episodes can be sustained, "Prisoner" might be the best, most rousing drama serial made in this country. The first show is stirring stuff, intelligently written and brilliantly acted. It's light years ahead of the other Grundy fodder, "The Young Doctors" and "The Restless Years".'

John Hanrahan, an experienced TV journalist (and now producer) wrote in the Sydney *Sun*: ' "Prisoner" will be the most powerful continuing drama on Australian television with no holds-barred scenes of prison riots, fights between prison staff and inmates, drugs and illicit affairs between staff and inmates.'

The most powerful outburst against 'Prisoner' in Australia came from a totally unexpected quarter, the Victorian Prisons Department, with jail psychiatrist Dr. Allan Bartholomew condemning the show as being 'sadistic and grotesque'. He wanted the series axed. 'I hope it receives poor ratings. I've been counselling women prisoners for twenty years but have never come across such sadism and depravity as portrayed in this series.'

Dr. Bartholomew, president of the Australian and New Zealand Society of Criminology, said the series was morally dangerous. 'The Correctional Services have worked for years to achieve public recognition for a valuable task well performed. Programmes like "Prisoner" only undermine morals.'

The Governor of the Fairlea Women's Prison Committee was also a volatile critic. Dame Phyllis Frost accused Grundy's of not consulting authorities on life in the women's prisons. But producer Ian Bradley was quick to explain Grundy's had approached women's prison officials on several occasions and suggested the appointment of a prison officer to ensure authenticity in the series.

'Grundy's thought the appointment of a liaison officer was an excellent idea and backed it from the start,' said Bradley. 'But the prison officials wouldn't come to the party, even though they knew we were intent on making the show as realistic as possible. We started talks with the authorities more than six months before the first episodes of "Prisoner" went to air. They had some suggestions for the opening episodes which we previewed to them. After that they just failed to show any interest at all. Yet we have had two former women prisoners acting as consultants on the series from the start.'

Later, the always outspoken morals crusader, Rev. Fred Nile, of the Festival of Light, railed against the serial at a hearing for Channel Ten's licence renewal in Sydney. 'It emphasised terror and violence, depicted illicit sex acts and had objectionable

PRISONER FILE

Name: Maxine Daniels

Actress: Lisa Crittenden

Maxine had been caught up in criminal activities for a long time with a notorious gang. She is finally nabbed during a robbery. Some of Maxine's traits were not too appealing to actress Lisa Crittenden. 'I'm terrified of motorbikes and I don't like the tattoos. I had to wear one on each arm. The make-up people put them on every day -- thank goodness, I could wash them off again at night.'

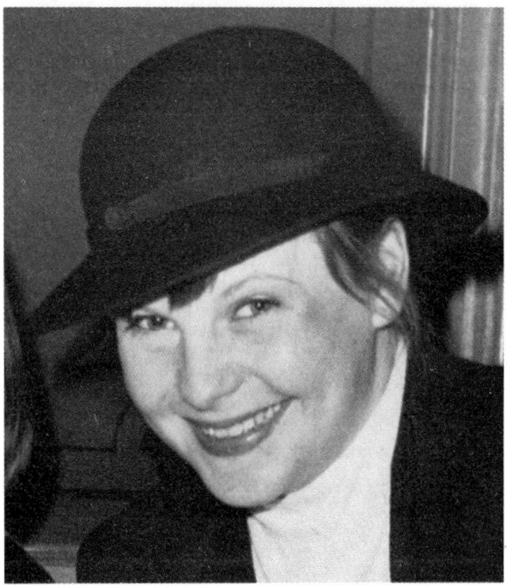

Solo

language.' Secretly, the producers and Channel Ten bosses thought it one of the best unpaid promotions the show had enjoyed.

But, generally, the critics and reviewers were impressed and willing to give 'Prisoner' a chance. The jail officials were seen to have a vested interest and their complaints would play second fiddle to what the journalists wrote in the nation's columns.

The *Daily Mirror*'s (Sydney) entertainment writer, Matt White, went straight to the point with his review of the opening episodes. 'Women individually are usually charming and delightful creatures. Collectively they can be bitches. Cage them together and you have a hell-house of appalling animalistic behaviour which would revolt the meanest animals. This jaundiced view of the fairer sex is grimly amplified in "Prisoner".

'As the title suggests it is about jailbirds – by birds, I mean of the human female variety – and what you see and hear about them is not very nice. It is powerful stuff, with top acting and a memorable theme song, "On the Inside", sung by Lynne Hamilton.'

PRISONER FILE

Name: Dr. Kate Petersen

Actress: Olivia Hamnett

Olivia Hamnett is a tall, elegant British actress with scores of TV roles to her credit as well as playing the mother of Ricky Schroeder in The Earthling *(1980) and Richard Chamberlain's wife in* The Last Wave *(1977).*

Dr. Kate Petersen was an intellectual -- and so ostracised by most inmates. She was also a convicted murderer, the poisoner of her lover. At first viewers found her 'so nice' but she soon showed her true colours. 'She's a devious and cunning person who will try to ingratiate herself with the other prisoners,' said Olivia when she joined the cast. 'There's no brawn about Dr. Kate so she has to use all of her wit and wiles.'

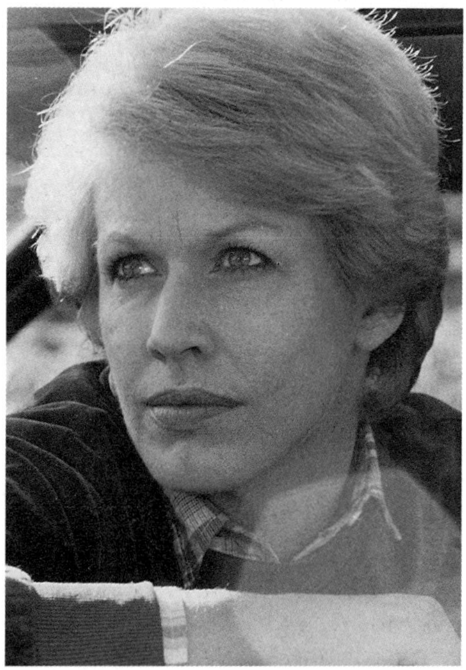

The only consistent criticism was limited to the background of schoolteacher killer Karen Travers's dilemma. The prison doctor finds her back covered with cigarette burns obviously inflicted by her late husband, the unfaithful louse she scissored to death in the famous shower scene, though there was no mention of the burns in her defence during the trial which sent her to Wentworth. But 'Prisoner' soon settled down winning viewers with its realism and grit.

Commenting on lissome Lynn Warner's predicament, *National Times* TV writer Michael Le Moignan observed, 'Lynn is played by Kerry Armstrong with smouldering innocence and the sort of "save me" eyes knights used to fight dragons for. A fresh young country girl, she came to the city to work as a nanny, only to be unjustly accused by her mistress of burying the infant alive. Now, both her appearance and acting make it quite clear Lynn could have no more buried a baby than Snow White could have machine-gunned the Seven Dwarfs. But rather than leave a dramatic subtlety without hammering it to pieces, we were provided with a macabre close-up of the Wicked Queen in the shape of Lynn's ex-employer leering into the baby's cot threatening to put the infant "back in that big hole" if it didn't stop crying.'

TV Soap editor-publisher Ben Mitchell commented, 'Any show that starts with a shower stabbing, goes on to a suicide and a prison brawl, has lesbians on parade, an assault in a laundry, a roly-poly girl inmate who sucks her fingers and cuddles a teddy bear and a grizzled old lady who chain-smokes and is a kleptomaniac can't be too bad. But can they keep it up?'

Several previewers made the mistake of asking Carol Burns if she had any affinity with the world of wildcat Franky Doyle. It always prompted the same horrified reply. 'No! No way. She's stupid, vicious, she can't read, she's violent, and no one cares for her.'

But viewers in their strange way would care for Franky. She quickly drew droves of admirers and supporters, especially when the scripts began explaining her background and slowly unravelled her psychotic personality.

'Prisoner's' first producer, Ian Bradley, was aware the show had a good chance of maintaining its high expectations. 'We were doing a show a week to begin with, then upped it to two shows, and we made sure our writers had the time to do the job. We had to stay fresh, original and powerful.'

Reg Watson, usually a background figure at launches or awards nights, because he likes his colleagues to have the limelight, found himself much in demand as the first night's telecast neared. 'I started it off, but they did all the work.' Watson confidently predicted a successful future for his latest creation. 'I don't see the prisons emptying,' he said at the final press preview.

Previews over, with generally good press, it was now only a matter of days before the Australian public would have its say. There'd been a secret telephone survey – nothing unusual for new shows or product-testing in most English-language TV markets

– in advance of the officially sanctioned and industry-financed McNair Anderson ratings. And the champagne was out on the set of 'Prisoner' at its Nunawading base.

Max Stewart, station boss of Channel O, and his programme chief, Gordon French, came on set to help celebrate, along with elated publicists George Wilson and Eileen O'Shea. Among the most prized callers for a job well done were Ten Sydney boss, Ian Kennon, Ten PR maestro Brian Walsh, Grundy chiefs, Ian Holmes and Reg Watson, and their Sydney PR lady, Felicity Goscombe.

Even Reg Grundy took time out to make sure his hard-working cast and crew knew their winning form was greatly appreciated at Grundy's highest level of management. He sent congratulatory best wishes from his Los Angeles enclave via Ian Holmes.

The official ratings confirmed what everyone now knew – 'Prisoner' was a runaway hit. Rival networks realised they were faced with a tough challenge as the unlimited nitty-gritty stories at Wentworth rolled off the wordprocessors. The storylines for 'Prisoner' seemed to get more daring week-by-week as the main core of characters battled their way through the vigorous routines of everyday life in Wentworth Detention Centre. Few prison stones were left unturned as Grundy researchers and writers thrived on the show's quick success with about one and a half million regular viewers in Sydney and Melbourne.

The writers threw in everything they could think of. The pace of the show was fast and fierce. The format welcomed that sort of 'hit 'em fast, hit 'em hard' attitude Watson wanted. 'What their research and familiarity didn't dig up for the ongoing brutalities and rampant violence, they made up. Nothing wrong with that in soaps. That's the true form of story-telling,' wrote a Sydney journalist.

One thing was patently clear to O-TEN and Grundy's. 'Prisoner' had gathered a large following. It was a major hit from day one and they were buoyed by slogans like: '1980 – Year of Prisoner'.

Even the usually high-brow TV column of *The Australian*'s Suellen O'Grady worried about the frantic pace. Ms O'Grady wrote: 'Murder, muggings and brawls are joyous affairs for the female inmates of Wentworth Detention Centre. No neurotic doubts plague these women as they thrust pairs of scissors into unsuspecting backs or

PRISONER FILE

Name: Susie Driscoll

Actress: Jacqui Gordon

Susie Driscoll managed to behave herself well enough inside Wentworth to get parole. But when she went to work in a fast food restaurant, she found her past catching up with her.

20-year-old Jacqui Gordon played Susie. Jacqui is the step-daughter of veteran Australian actor Vic Gordon, who played Albert Kennedy in 'Matlock Police'.

pull guns out of chocolate boxes to shoot their husbands. No looks of even momentary guilt flicker across their faces as the blood begins to spill, only smiles fit for people who have just won $1 million.

'Because of the lack of conversation and glut of action, there is no time to blink or blow one's nose or a vital murder or mugging could be missed. "Prisoner" is certainly entertaining, if improbable, viewing. The one problem is, can O-TEN keep up the pace for the remaining forty or so episodes? Or, more to the point, can we?'

One critic came unstuck when he observed: 'Two female inmates are serving time in solitary in adjoining cells. Now, if we're to believe anything about "Prisoner", it should be that it is a real prison. Real prisons have thick walls to keep prisoners in, yet these two recalcitrants were having a very chummy talk despite the very thick walls between them. You try it!'

Real-life prisoner Tim Anderson, biding time in Matraville Central Industrial Prison in Sydney, wrote in reply to the Sydney *Sun-Herald* that the show 'had many artificial elements, not the least of them is that the prison set looks nothing like a real prison. However, talking through walls in solitary confinement isn't quite as impossible as you might think. The best form of communication is through water pipes or the toilet system: this is "the phone". Ventilation ducts, windows and doors all add to the possibilities. One good thing should be said about "Prisoner" is that it has helped create a greater sense of public sympathy for prisoners. If the programme helps the public relate to us as human beings rather than the faceless monsters that many authorities like to portray, then it is certainly having a good effect.' (Tim Anderson was one of three Ananda Marga sect members charged with the bomb deaths of two Sydney City Council garbagemen and a policeman when an explosion took place outside the Hilton Hotel during an Asian prime minister's conference in 1979. The three defendants served seven years in jail before the New South Wales State Government set them free and quashed the convictions. Within fourteen months Anderson was again charged with the bombings and at the time of writing is again claiming his innocence at a trial.)

About 150 verifiable letters were received by O-TEN and Grundy's from inmates in both men's and women's jails in the opening six weeks of the show, and most of them

P R I S O N E R F I L E

Name: Donna Mason

Actress: Arkie Whiteley

Donna Mason is on skid row when she is admitted to Wentworth and dependent on drugs sneaked into jail. Donna is played by Arkie Whiteley, the daughter of acclaimed Australian artist, Brett Whiteley. Born in England, she travelled the world as a child with, during her time in the U.S.A., a very unusual baby-sitter -- Janis Joplin.

were happy with the drama and had quickly warmed to the characters. The only general theme of criticism was that real jail life was much more boring than that portrayed in 'Prisoner'.

Several letters arrived from former or current residents of orphanages and boarding schools, saying 'Prisoner' had struck a chord with them too. The general gist of the mail, was that the show brought back memories or paralleled present lives in those institutions, 'which seemed a sad indictment of the places,' wrote Don Groves (Sydney *Sun-Herald*).

Up north in the sunshine State of Queensland the law enforcers and moralists did a quick hatchet job on 'Prisoner'. Ironically, ten years later, the Fitzgerald Commission would prove many of Queensland's top-ranking state politicians and senior policeman had spent twenty years raking off millions of dollars in prostitution and nightclub protection rackets, real estate and land development deals and abuse of governmental inflated petty cash claims. In the meantime, 'Prisoner' was banned from screens in Queensland prisons, branded as 'cheap, degrading, sensational, squalid and without any redeeming features'. Similar words would be used to describe some of the thirty-five politicians and policemen at the Fitzgerald Inquiry.

Surprisingly, back down in the South, there were penal reform activists in Prisoner's home state of Victoria who wanted the show outlawed from their prisons. Sanity, however, prevailed, and a lengthy and often boisterous meeting between representatives from the State Government Corrective Services division – including Pentridge and Fairlea Prisons - and Grundy's and Channel O took place in Melbourne on 7 March 1979. Community Welfare Services Minister, Brian Dixon, confirmed the series would 'continue to be available to Victorian prisoners with access to TV sets', but he stressed the meeting regarded the first three episodes of 'Prisoner' as 'an exaggerated and distorted coverage of real life in prison'.

PRISONER FILE

Name: Camellia Wells

Actress: Annette Andre

Annette Andre's first break as an actress was as Elizabeth Taylor's handmaiden in Cleopatra. *While in the U.K. in the Seventies, she was a regular in* Emergency Ward 10 *and* Randall and Hopkirk, *and just as regularly hit the headlines when she dated millionaire matador El Cordobes and soccer star George Best. In 'Prisoner' she plays sophisticated talk show hostess, Camellia Wells, jailed for not paying a parking fine.*

DOCUMENTARY EVIDENCE

'Prisoner' created headlines in the Melbourne press in late June with the discovery by actors and crew of confidential police and court documents.

The documents, found in an abandoned suburban courthouse and police station which Grundy's rented regularly for shooting, contained several hundred names and addresses and other personal details. They covered a wide range of offences, including car and traffic infringements, non-payment of bills, prostitution and theft. Police cells at the Prahran Courthouse complex were stacked several feet high with varied books, receipts, court orders, bail books, police reports and, financial papers. On the day they notified the Prahran Council of scattered files at the location premises, the crew spent nearly an hour removing general rubbish, sorting files into half-empty boxes before cleaning the courtroom to start rehearsing trial scenes involving Elspeth Ballantyne.

Prahran Council and the Crown Law Department sent officials to the courthouse soon after the calls were made to complain about the messy files. No more was heard of the matter. 'It was all hushed up,' revealed a 'Prisoner' crew member. 'That night there was a huge clean-up. Government vans took everything away the next day.'

The softer side of everyone at Wentworth comes to the fore in a poignant storyline that has the inmates organising a fund-raising appeal for six-year-old deaf girl Debbie Peters (played so well by Anna Crawford, daughter of Crawford's Productions managing director Ian Crawford and his charming wife Mercedes). To make her role more authentic, Anna went to the Princess Elizabeth Junior School for the Deaf to learn sign language. 'Now she's teaching it to kids at her own school,' said Mercedes.

It got to the stage that you never knew who would pop up on the screen as 'Prisoner' headed towards its record-breaking 500th episode. Ultra-marathon runner, 53-year-old Cliff Young, appeared on the show as himself, tutoring the inmates on fitness as they organised an attempt to break the world record of 72 hours waltzing to raise funds for little deaf girl Debbie Peters. Potato-farmer Cliff hit the headlines when he won the inaugural Sydney-Melbourne marathon (600 miles) in 1982 with his famous 'gum-boot shuffle' gait.

7

THE FIRST INMATES

Carol Burns had a soft spot for the boisterous, misshapen Franky Doyle, as did the fans – the avalanche of mail from Australian and American viewers proved that. 'I loved the character from the very first time I saw the scripts. I thought it was probably the best television part for any woman in Australian TV. I felt for Franky, even though she was totally aggressive, and unloved through her own stupidity. She was human and, in her own way, honest.'

Two major admissions from Carol: 'I didn't go to any prisons to research Franky, and I'd never talked to a bikie before in my life. But after a couple of weeks on the show I met one on a beach and ended up buying him a beer in the local pub. I also met a woman in a Wollongong (an industrial city near Sydney) hospital having tattoos removed.'

No sooner was she an established favourite than Carol Burns asked for her role to be terminated. It was 8 March 1979 when the news broke, but Franky would be seen on screen for another five months as the Wentworth gang was then shooting Episode Twenty-six and into a two-shows-a-week schedule. Carol said she couldn't keep the pace.

Producer Bradley said, 'We have had to schedule extra shootings and agree with Carol that it would be difficult for her to continue playing Franky at this high standard. Carol is a very versatile actress. She takes a lot of time to get into her part and works very hard at it. Perhaps we can write her back into the show at a later date.'

But Carol had reached the stage where she wanted out, and asked that 'Franky go out with a bang – dead, gone and buried.' She got her wishes and the mourning around the country and in the United States added to the Franky Doyle cult society.

Carol was so affected by an immediate deluge of mail, telephone calls and even petitions asking that she reconsider and stay in Wentworth, that she made an unprecedented and emotional appearance on 'The Steve Raymond Show' to explain why she had to leave. 'It was almost as hard as playing Franky in full flight, but I had made up my mind and, while I was very touched by the support of so many fans, there was no new reason to reassess the situation or change my mind.'

Carol's resignation meant that top Australian movie actor, Jack Thompson, wouldn't be seen in the series either. Jack (star of the popular World War II 'Spyforce' series and the movies *Sunday Too Far Away, Breaker Morant, Scobie Malone, Petersen*) had wanted to work with Carol in 'Prisoner', playing off the character of Franky Doyle. This meant Jack was going back to TV after refusing small-screen work for years. Jack

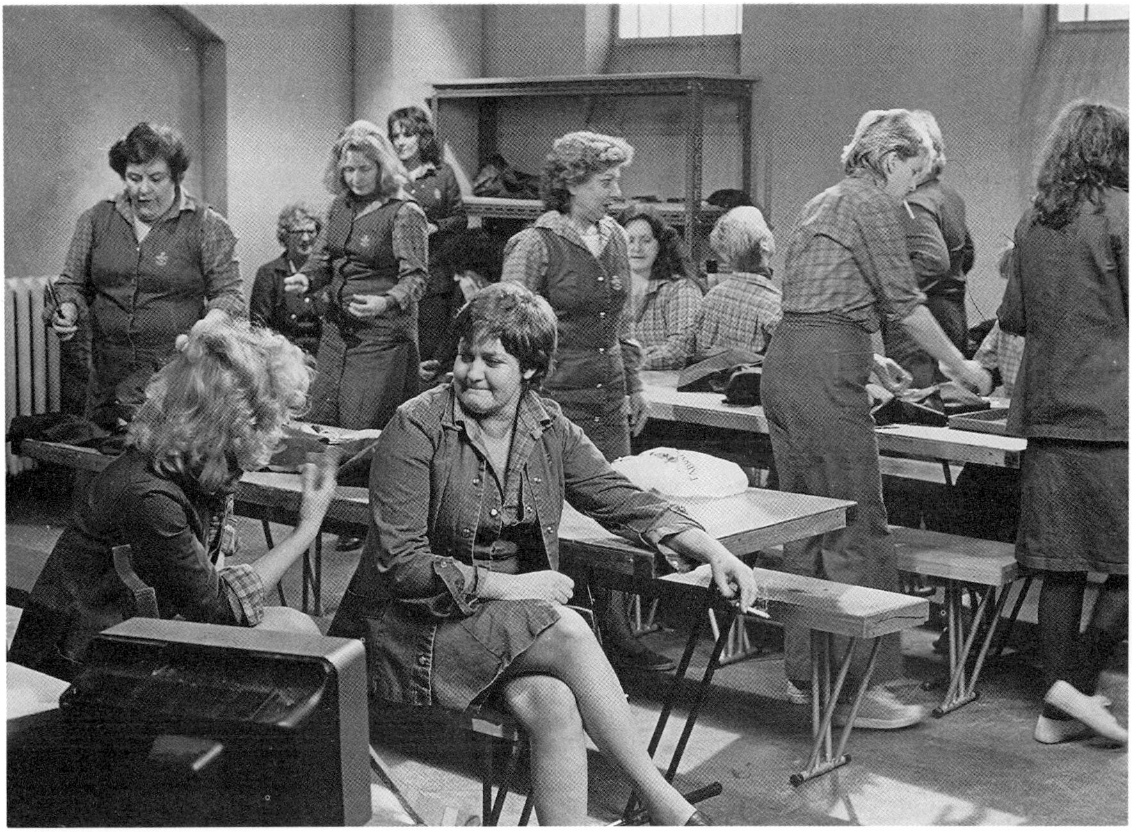

Tea-break in the canteen for the Wentworth girls as Chrissie Latham (Amanda Muggleton, back to camera) chats with Bea Smith (Val Lehman)

had met Carol when she was 14. They were involved with local theatre groups in Brisbane and it was Jack who did most to encourage Carol's career.

Grundy's responded by changing the emphasis to the Bea Smith character, ably carried on Val Lehman's strong shoulders, and they increased Sheila Florance's workload, too. The writers also started to build up Elspeth Ballantyne's role of warder Meg Morris. And there was a steady influx of new faces in the cells and in uniform.

American actress Betty Bobbitt, 31, who had first come to Australia in 1962 at the invitation of the Seven Network to work as a featured artist on the 'Daly At Night' show with American comics Jonathon Daly and Ken Delo, soon made an impression as inmate Judy Bryant. Bryant was on a marijuana possession charge, and set to get a bond and fine. But she missed her lover, Sharon Gilmore (Margot Knight), and made sure she stayed in Wentworth with Sharon by getting caught with marijuana in the lock-up. The ruse worked. According to Betty's contract she would be doing porridge for two months. But the Judy Bryant character was an immediate success and Betty would end up on a five-year acting stretch.

In the years between 'Daly' and 'Prisoner', Betty's resonant voice and 'Yank, then mid-Atlantic accent' kept her in demand much of the time and brought her many solid acting jobs. But she admits there were desperate times in 1967 and '68 when she moved to Sydney to work in the computer mailing business (the lowest point of my life). She was in the 1976 movie, *Eliza Frazer*, starring Susannah York, Noel Ferrier and Trevor Howard. Betty's TV credits included 'Bellbird', 'Matlock Police' and 'Cop Shop'. And she was a regular contract player for the acclaimed Melbourne Theatre Company. She also hit the high spots as a member of the Glitter Sisters singing duo.

'I made sure Judy was portrayed as having a kindly, sensitive side. The lesbian aspects of "Prisoner" were fairly heavy and overdone in the early days, but Judy was a much more realistic and honest version of that breed,' said Betty.

Beautiful blonde Briony Behets, 27, was the next major inmate to check into Wentworth. Only weeks before, the British-born actress's latest movie, *Long Weekend*, starring John Hargreaves as her husband, had been unveiled to good notices. The ecological thriller was written and directed by Bri's boyfriend, Colin Eggleston, a driving force behind some of Crawford Productions' drama output in the late Sixties and Seventies.

Briony was one of the original sexpots in 'Number 96', and did a 14-month stint as Judy Donovan in 'The Box' series. A former teacher, she'd been in Australia since 1972, when she co-starred in the bizarre rat attack thriller *Night of Fear*, and had a high profile as Tuesday in the TV series 'Birds in the Bush' (U.K. title: 'Virgin Fellas'). In 'Prisoner' she was compulsive shoplifter Susan Rice, mother of two, whose unstable marriage led her to crime. Her six-week story was shown from the traumatic clashes at home through to her arrest and arrival at Wentworth.

'I have turned down a lot of soap offers over the past two years,' explained Briony, 'to try and get away from sex-oriented roles. The years catch up with you, and I really want to do more dramatic work, even if it's support or guest pieces.'

The workload told on all the main players. Most lived in Melbourne and could get away from the rigours of making the show simply by driving home. It was different and more difficult for the inter-state Sydney cast. They tried to get home as regularly as possible. Some made it two or three times a month, others once a month. It depended on the state of the heart and pocket – 500 miles of the treacherous Hume Highway took their toll on car and driver, and the one-hour commercial jet flight cost a packet (up to $295 (£140) return by the time the show ended in 1986).

Extra characters would soon be introduced in an effort to lessen the pressures on the regular players and it had been decided that men would be featured more prominently, too.

Mary Ward was the next regular to depart her cell at Wentworth. 'It's sad,' the veteran actress revealed, 'but two shows a week are taking their toll on me. It would be all right if I was younger. But that's the penalty you pay when the years catch up with you. I've loved doing the role of Mum Brookes, and all the girls in the show have been wonderful. They've treated me real nice. I haven't been killed off, so maybe I'll be back sometime. I would like that, but right now I'm off to Perth to see my family and friends and have a rest after a year in clink.'

The writers took a simple way out for gardening-fanatic Mum's exit. They wrote in an on-screen heart-attack and rushed her off to an emergency hospital for specialised

Chorus line at a Prisoner cast concert (*from left*): Bea Smith (Val Lehman), Judy Bryant (Betty Bobbitt), Doreen Campbell (Colette Mann), Lizzie Birdsworth (Sheila Florance) and Margot Gaffney (Jane Clifton). Bobbitt, Mann and Clifton sang professionally as a group, The Mini-Busettes

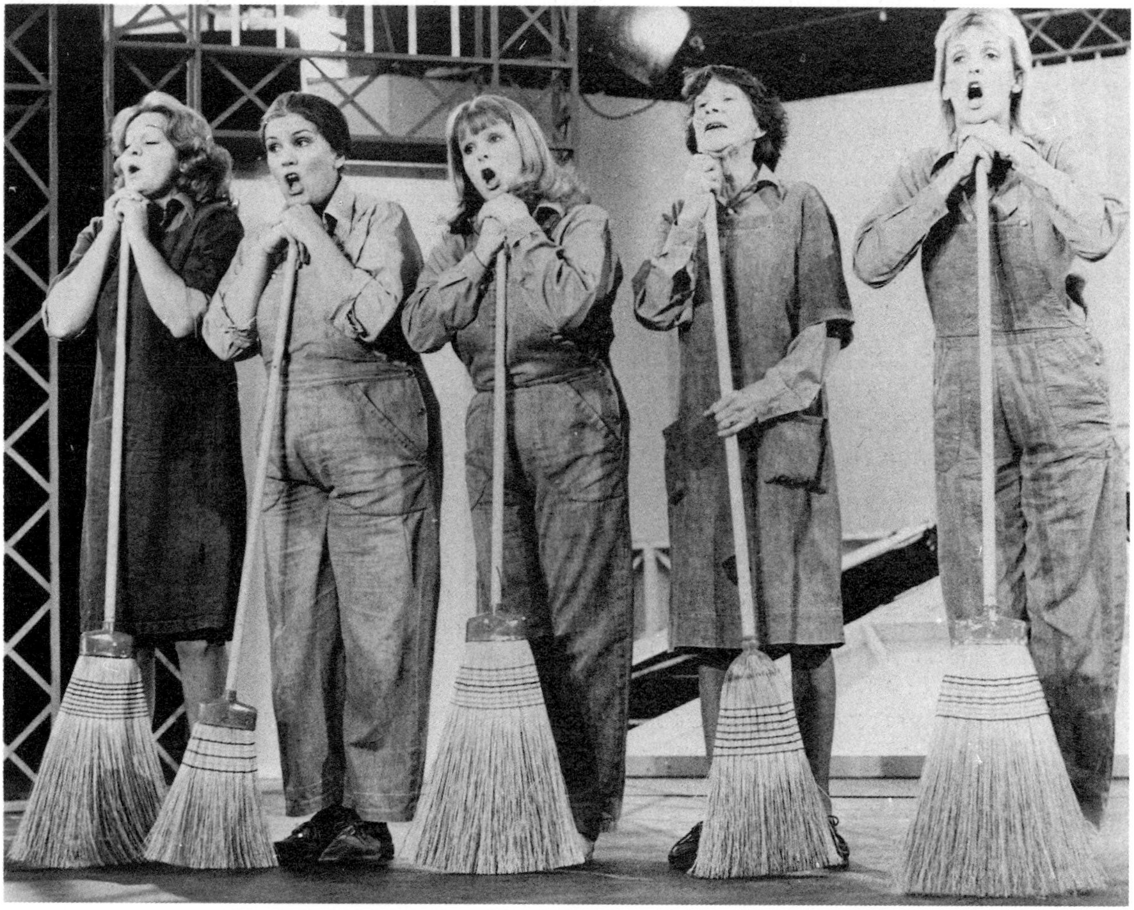

A DAY IN THE TUNNEL

It was a long, hard slog producing the two hours of 'Prisoner' each week. The cast started rehearsal at around 8 a.m. on Mondays, Tuesdays and Wednesda$s, usually on a ten-hour call, and then they would tape for up to fourteen hours a day on Thursday and Friday.

'Have a heavy night on the town, and you really pay for it the next morning,' said Val Lehman. 'You've really got to be on your toes and have a clear mind. No one has time to sit around and mope or nurse a hangover or headache, you can't take it easy. It's go, go, go.'

In between rehearsals and taping, the cast had the 'Tunnel' for relaxing – a sort of a Green Room (traditionally where actors relax before going on set). The Nunawading studio tunnel was a cosy set-up with posters and notices stuck on the walls. Coffee and tea was always on the boil, and at the end of the Tunnel, a giant settee and the start of the wardrobe department.

Usually the Tunnel was a bit of a mess, with chairs, pouffes, scripts, soft drink bottles, poly coffee cups, discarded clothing and wardrobe pieces. 'Who cares?' said Fiona Spence. 'It's comfortable, and we rush in and out during rehearsals and tapings. It's home.'

It was also where the cast got to read the latest PR sheets, mail from viewers and keep track of scripts and the regular changes. Even a book could come in handy – in between those incessant cigarettes Sheila Florance intently read a latest bestseller, while Colette Mann was just as studious, deep in notes for a forthcoming episode in which she would give the writers some advice and background information on inmate counselling. She also carried a few battered paperbacks.

Occasionally, there would be a speedy visit to the studio pay-phone, or a special trip to the make-up room for simulated blood or wounds.

The Tunnel was a place of constant activity except when the cameras were turning or rehearsals underway. Flowers, cards and gifts arrived regularly. Val Lehman was amused by one particular gift, a box of chocolates with a hidden bonus, a ten-inch hacksaw. 'The chocolates are great,' crooned Val, who then had to explain how she, Sheila, Colette and Fiona Spence had eaten the lot.

'They're like the Three Musketeers,' said a soundman. 'Val's the unofficial leader of Sheila and Colette. They're together all the time. They're a load of fun, great mates, and the crew love 'em – and can they tell jokes, most of which you could never put in print.'

Elspeth Ballantyne had missed out on the chocolate, but was busy telling an on-set visiting reporter that much of the appeal of 'Prisoner' comes from the fact that the women on screen aren't dolly-birds. 'Women can relate to us.'

When the subject of children, single-parenthood and mum's arduous schedules on 'Prisoner', Elspeth and Val were soon in earnest discussion.

Because of the long working hours, Elspeth zealously guarded her restricted time with children Matthew (11) and Tobias (9). Her career had taken a back seat soon after she married 'Bellbird' beau Denis Miller, one of Australia's busiest actors. She had raised the boys since the 1977 split from Miller. 'Naturally, there are unique problems coping as a single working mum, and "Prisoner" has changed my lifestyle.

With 'Prisoner' slotted into the 8.30 p.m. adult viewing time on the O-TEN Network the boys had yet to see their mum on TV. 'They asked me once if they could watch it, and I said certainly not. They tried to con their grandparents during a holiday in Adelaide, but Mum and Dad were always watching ABC, thankfully.'

Val Lehman also placed special priorities with her two girls, Cassie (16) and Joanne (15). 'My life away from Wentworth is fairly simple. We spend most of the free weekends on a farm owned by a close, close friend. All I can say is, I'm extremely happy.' Val divorced her Army officer husband. 'He thought there wasn't enough room in the family for two careers, so we broke up. Acting is something I couldn't give up.'

treatment and a long stay in an intensive care unit, which you wouldn't see on screen. That way, Mum could be left in limbo and retrieved for later episodes.

In any event, the garden wouldn't be the same without Mum. She'd helped plant those first seeds and her every spare moment had cultivated much of the colour and beauty in the small plot, which seemed so remote from the day-to-day life of Wentworth.

Wentworth's other older player, Sheila Florance, had her own unique ways of coping with the demands of Lizzie Birdsworth. Sheila rushes everywhere, as she has done all her life, which she says keeps her weight down. And she attributed her good health to a 'special diet' - stout and vegetables. She was drinking at least six small bottles of stout daily, devouring plenty of fresh vegetables, and 'swallowing a ton of vitamin pills a day'. Sheila claimed her only vice was a huge one – smoking. 'I just can't help it – it stops me from getting nervous.' Her sons Peter, Dean of the Victorian College of Drama, and Phillip, a TV cameraman, were always at their mum to quit. But to no avail.

'I can switch off from here,' she told *Daily Mirror* journalist Fran Hernon during an interview at the studios. 'I go home to my darling husband John and do the cooking. I love cooking.

'Our house is packed with memorabilia. I've lived a full, rich life and have a home full of mementos, each one has a story. In fact, I can remember who gave me each one of them. Not bad for an old dodderer of 63.'

Rosie Sturgess, a longstanding comedy favourite with Oz TV audiences, and respected stage and TV actress Monica Maughan, joined the 'Prisoner' ranks as a mother and daughter combination. Monica played Pat O'Connell, mother of two young children, jailed for aiding and abetting her husband and son in an armed robbery. Rosie played Pat's mum, Mrs Devlin, left at home to look after the fretting kids.

Viewers warmed to the two players – Rosie had been a big name in 'The Wilson Family' sketches on Graham Kennedy's 'In Melbourne Tonight', and as the long-suffering wife of Alwyn Kurts in 'The Last of the Australians', a 39-part series unashamedly copied from Warren Mitchell's U.K. show 'Till Death Us Do Part'.

Monica had been an Ozcar Best Actress movie winner for her poignant performance as a troubled spinster in the 1975 Melbourne movie *A City's Child*, and was well known to Australian TV viewers for her major role as office secretary Maureen Flaherty in 'The Box' series also shot at the Nunawading studios.

Towards the end of 1979, more new faces appeared before the cameras at Wentworth. Some would be seen on air before the December end-of-season episode, with the others filtering through the first months of 1980.

Doreen would get a boyfriend and, after some serious courting, the possibility of wedding bells. Ros Speirs, 28, a tall sophisticated actress best known for her splendid work as Nellie West, wife of the central character in the powerful ABC-TV series 'Power Without Glory', and later to become an actors' agent, was arriving as new prisoner Caroline Simpson, on remand for the stabbing murder of her woman-bashing father. The unusual arrival of Caroline was compounded by the company of her distraught mother (Bernadette Hillier), also charged with the killing. Caroline's presence in everyday clothing – she was never a regular inmate – set her aside from the other prisoners, and she had to suffer their mistrust. She would get 'slightly involved' with Deputy Governor Jim Fletcher (Gerard Maguire).

PRISONER FILE

Name: Nola McKenzie
Actress: Carol Skinner

Dual killer, Nola McKenzie, was on death row in Western Australia for the murder of her husband and a prison guard when she broke out -- and ended up in custody at Wentworth with an armed robbery charge. For actress Carol Skinner, 38, it was the biggest challenge of her career. 'I'd never played a genuine nasty before. Nola's tough, evil and deadly -- there isn't an ounce of human compassion in her. She hasn't a good word for anyone and she's absolutely hideous to poor old Lizzie.'

PRISONER FILE

Name: Roxanne Laporte
Actress: Peppie d'Or

Peppie d'Or, 22, was no newcomer to Australian soap, having previously appeared in 'Cop Shop', 'Holiday Island' and 'The Sullivans'. Normally, her presence meant glitz and glamour -- but for 'Prisoner' she had to appear seven months pregnant.

Even Bea Smith, now undisputed boss of the cells in the wake of Franky Doyle's death, was in the arms of reformed ex-con Ken Pearce (played by Tom Oliver) and tugging at the audience's heart-strings.

Sigrid Thornton was the next classical beauty to boost 'Prisoner's glamour stakes, a 23-year-old Queenslander who was being touted as a international star because of her classic cheekbones, big brown eyes and undeniable screen chemistry. She'd appeared with Patrick Cargill in 'Father, Dear Father, Down Under', 'Homicide' and 'The Sullivans', and made a promising cross to the big screen in *The Getting of Wisdom* (1977), *F. J. Holden* (1977) and *Snapshot* (1979). By coincidence, she would later star with Val Lehman in ABC-TV's 'Outbreak of Love'. In private life Sigrid lived with film producer-assistant director Tom Burstall and together they were renovating historical stables as a new home in an inner Melbourne suburb. Tom's British-born director-dad Tim was one of the movie-makers who led Australia's 1960s and '70s cinema resurgences (*Stork, 2000 Weeks, Alvin Purple, Last of the Knucklemen*).

Wentworth's assembly ogled the spunky new inmate for many different reasons from the moment she signed in as murderess Rosalyn Coulson, known to have strong ties with a group of militants. Ros might have been young, but she was a very complex person, and behind her attractive façade were uncontrollable, fiery demons.

In one of the most ambitious and daring plots of the series, Rosalyn's armed militia mates formulate an escape plan which would have done Charles Bronson or Sylvester Stallone proud. Armed to the teeth, Ros's renegades brought terrorism to Wentworth. Although Ros was blasted out of jail, her freedom would last only a few weeks.

Meanwhile off screen, the real-life romance of Barry Quin and Peta Toppano had blossomed. While playing roles as lovers in 'Prisoner' (he as caring Doctor Greg Miller, and she, inmate Karen Travers) they'd fallen in love and married quietly in April. Four months later they announced they were quitting. The script writers had ample time to wrap up their respective stories – Karen's retrial (owing much to Greg's loving persistence, and a skilful lawyer, played by Jim Smillie) resulted in her joining a work release programme. The knowing judge took into account Karen had already served eighteen months in custody, and new evidence showed she had been terrorised and scarred by her husband's brutal onslaughts before she attacked him with the scissors in the infamous shower scene.

As 1979 ended, Karen, courtesy of the scriptwriters, would be at death's door, requiring a rare and delicate operation – and who better to perform the life-giving surgery than Dr Greg? 1980 would see Karen on the outside.

Within days of finishing their work at Wentworth in late October, the happy couple were jetting to England to meet Barry's parents in Sussex. 'Barry and I need more time to get to know each other. We've had to live day and night with "Prisoner" all year. I really feel like Karen Travers – I'm out, free. I can smell the fresh air. It's wonderful,' Peta said just before taking the flight out of Sydney.

Early November revealed some of the inmates at Fairlea Women's Prison were modelling themselves on characters in 'Prisoner'. 'And the results are not very beneficial,' claimed Dame Phyllis Frost, convenor of the Fairlea Women's Prison

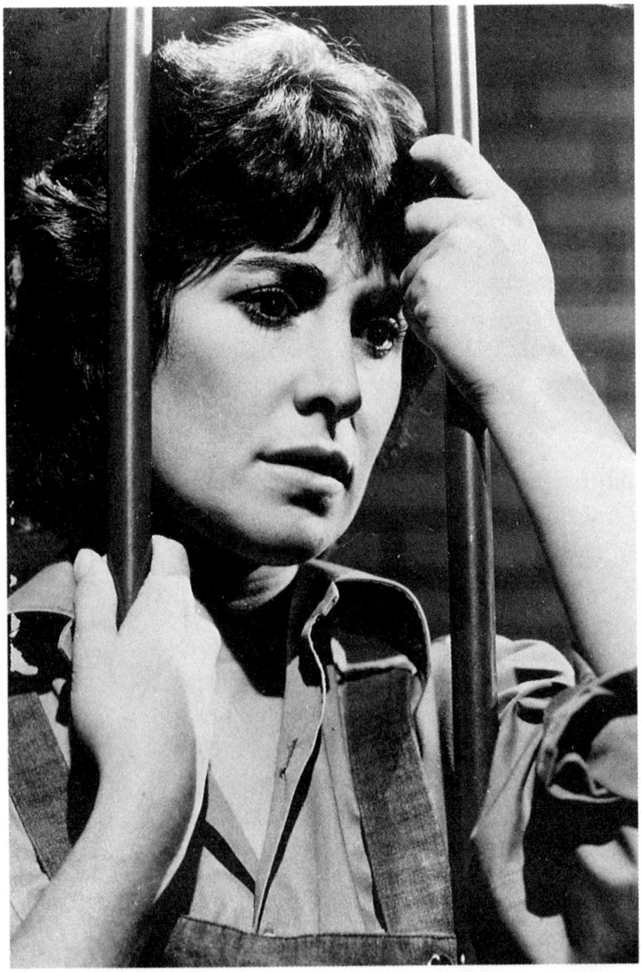

Karen Travers (Peta Toppano) was an ordinary, devoted school-teacher until she took a kitchen knife and stabbed her husband to death in the shower. A spine-tingling flashback to the famous scene in *Psycho*

PRISONER FILE

Name: Pixie Mason
Actress: Judy McBurney

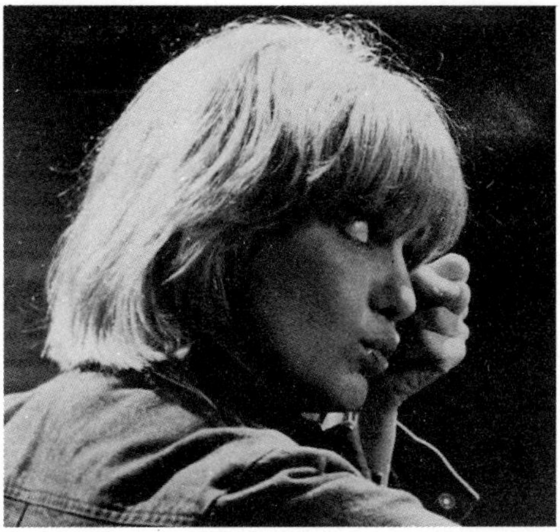

Sydney actress Judy McBurney was one of the most popular stars from 'The Young Doctors' where she played Tania Livingstone. As Pixie Mason, Network O-TEN's executive producer, Matt Carroll, called her 'a big character -- crazy and caught up in bigamy and fraud with a comic edge'. When male inmates arrive at Wentworth, Pixie is raped by Frank Bourke (Trevor Kent), setting off a chain reaction of brutal retaliations by Myra Desmond (Anne Phelan).

Council. As a result of the series, some of the women were at times endeavouring to act out roles depicted on screen, even adopting the names of the main prisoners and warders from Wentworth. The jail officials found it most disturbing that certain inmates had to be ordered 'in vigorous manner' to stop their charades and resume life as their former selves. Said a Fairlea official, 'It adds so many problems to daily administration.'

The newly appointed Governor of Fairlea, Mr Leslie Curll, agreed with Dame Phyllis: ' "Prisoner" as a series gives the wrong impression about jail life.' And the Victorian Minister for Community Welfare Services said the public at large had to realise the nature of Victoria's jail population has 'changed so very dramatically. The proportion of prisoners serving long terms for crimes of violence has almost doubled in the past ten years.'

One of those changes was reflected in the story of Caroline Simpson (Ros Speirs). She and her mum finally got their day in court and told how old man Simpson had beaten his wife for years. As the two women had already spent several months in Wentworth on remand, they were given suspended sentences on lesser charges of involuntary manslaughter. But Caroline had to agree to spend several weeks 'acclimatising in a halfway house', a fairly new experimental scheme in which trusted ex-prisoners and volunteer specialists helped newly released prisoners to face life with more confidence. (In later episodes Betty Bobbitt's character, Judy Bryant, would play a major role in setting up a halfway house with technical and personal advice from real-life ex-prisoner Sandra Willson.)

THE FRANKY DOYLE STORY

Given the strength of Franky Doyle's impact on audiences wherever 'Prisoner' was screened, Grundy's put a skilled team together to edit the lesbian bikie misfit's story into a two-hour special.

'The Franky Doyle Story' (what else?) replayed the more memorable events of her torrid stay at Wentworth, and, needless to say, was a gigantic hit. Flitting in and out of the special were the other regulars of the show, but the story was Franky's, and it didn't pause for breath along the way.

There was Franky's first romantic target, Karen Travers (Peta Toppano); the storm which erupted when Doreen Anderson (Colette Mann), Franky's child-like girlfriend, was about to be moved to another ward, triggering the legendary destruction scene in the prison library; the deadly top dog tussles with Bea Smith (Val Lehman); murder and blood-letting in the brawls and riots; and the hunger strike.

Who could forget Franky's traumatic sufferings and gradual decline in the harrowing times after the death of her kid brother? He was the one person she genuinely loved, but they couldn't be together. Finally, that fateful escape attempt with bumbling Doreen after Lizzie was stricken along the way and Franky's short-lived freedom before she shot a policeman and was then gunned down herself.

And who could forget Franky's defiant dying words, 'Bloody bastards!'

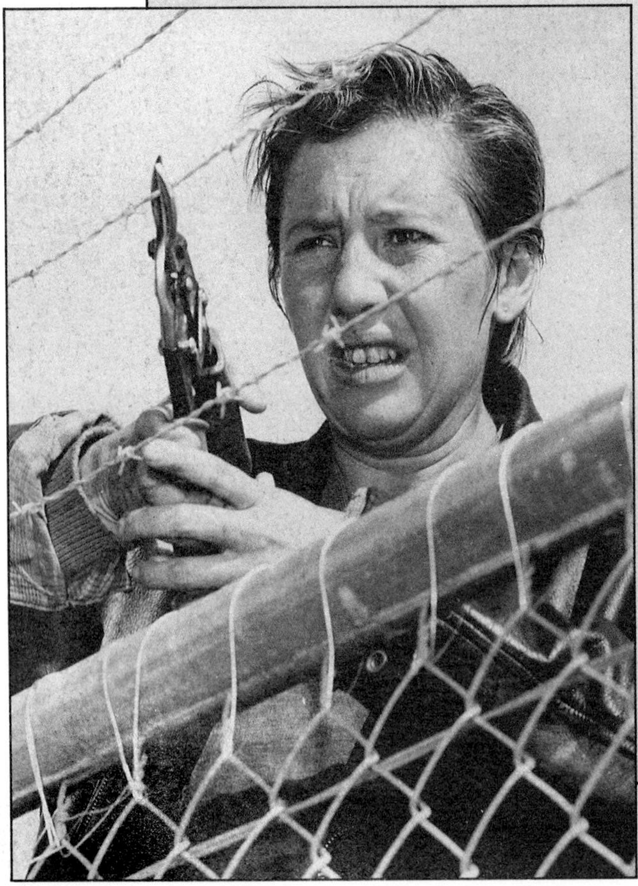

'The first part's easy' says Franky Doyle (Carol Burns) as she snips the barb-wire barring her escape from Wentworth. She is joined by Doreen Campbell (Colette Mann) and Lizzie Birdsworth (Sheila Florance)

There were critics, of course. Like the nationally mass circulated *TV Week* magazine, which questioned the patching together of a principal character's key scenes without giving proper and due consideration to other vital players.

Marion Macdonald wrote in her 'TV Extra' column in the highly respected *Sydney Morning Herald:* 'The producer has simply taken all the bits on Franky throughout the series and spliced them together, end-to-end, with ad-breaks to paper over the more remarkable leaps in narrative. This method is interesting in showing how the characters in a serial can be changed (from moronic to witty, for instance, from weak to steely) to fit the needs of the script or the prejudices of the scriptwriter. I can't think what else it has to recommend it.'

But the fans loved it and the ratings went through the roof. It was said to be the most VCR-copied telemovie of its time.

Franky Doyle (Carol Burns) about to go on the rampage in the canteen. She has the attention of Karen Travers (Peta Toppano) and Chrissie Latham (Amanda Muggleton (*centre*) but Old Lizzie Birdsworth (Sheila Florance), (*second from left*) has seen it all before

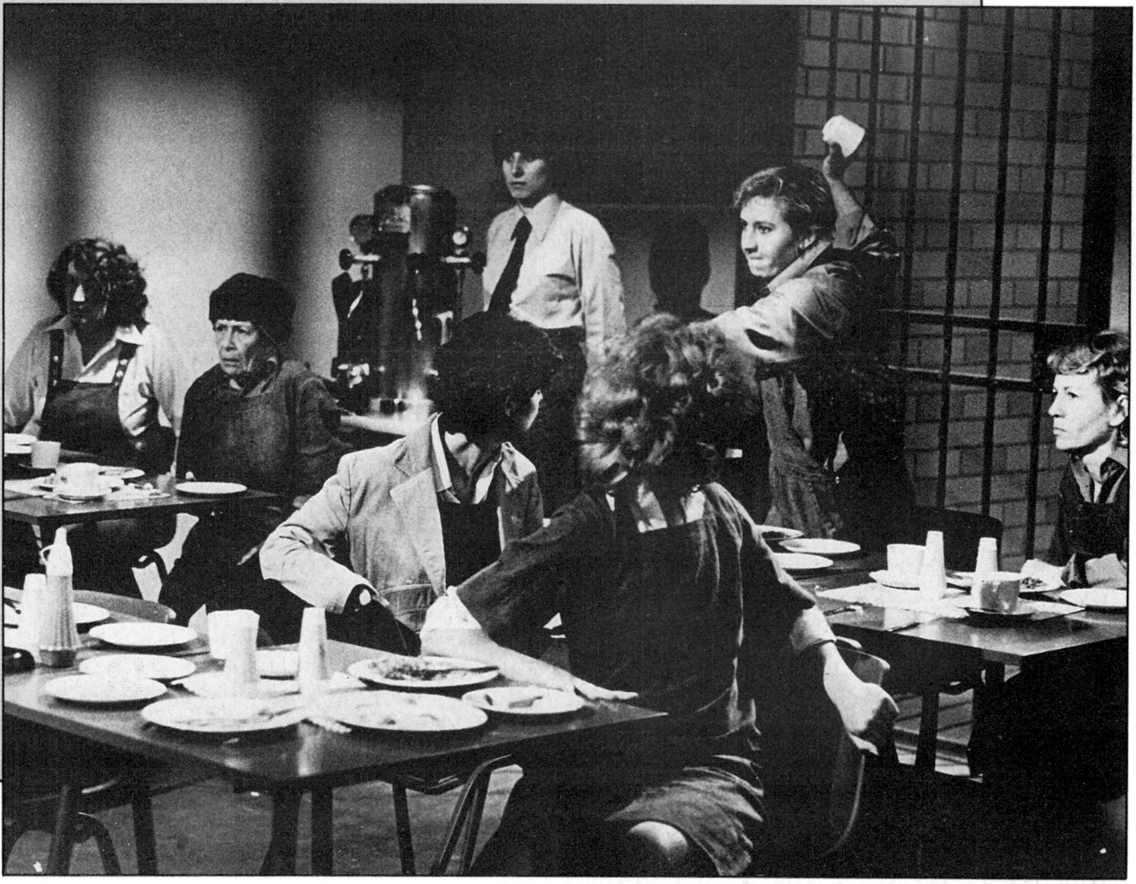

8

RECOGNITION AND IMITATION

'Prisoner's 100th episode went on the air in Sydney on 24 March 1980. In double wins at the prestigious *TV Week* Logie Awards (Australia's equivalent to the U.S. Emmys) 'Prisoner' was named Best Drama Series and Carol Burns given a standing ovation when presented with the award for Best Actress in a Drama Series.

'Prisoner' was now firmly established as one of the most watched shows in Australia, and its increasing American fan mail showed the same success there. About 45,000 signed photocards had been issued by cast members in less than six months, but the mail volume 'just got out of control. It hurt,' Colette Mann said at the time. 'We all found fan mail interesting and comforting at first. Most of us made time in the tunnel or at home to answer as many letters as possible. I wrote nearly eighty letters and autographed as many photos in one week. It was the same with the other girls – and we felt obliged to do it for the fans, for the show. But it got too big, too much, and it hurt because we were letting down the fans, the viewers.

'We could hardly keep up with the publicity. Everyone wanted to interview us. And more and more of the weekends were being taken up by promotional commitments. It wasn't hard to see we were well and truly trapped, "Prisoners of the pen", Sheila called us one day.'

Fans wanted to know all about their stars, who were now getting the type of blanket publicity coverage that hadn't been seen in Oz since 'Number 96'. But 'Number 96' hadn't seen the light of day overseas, unlike 'Prisoner's American cult following.

There was a slight hiccup in public relations for the show in August 1980, when a small group of Victorian State Police officers claimed they were concerned about the fast-growing violence on locally produced TV shows. They called for police to stop giving logistical assistance, manpower, traffic control support, technical advice and wardrobe or uniforms liaison to make shows like 'Prisoner' and the Crawford-produced 'Cop Shop'. The small clique of officers put their motion to the annual conference of the Victoria Police Association, but didn't get any worthwhile support.

Inspector Ted Rippon, secretary of the Association, said TV shows made overseas depicted far more sex, violence and horror than any Australian product. He personally could see no reason to withdraw longstanding liaison and support. 'And I watch both "Cop Shop" and "Prisoner",' said the police boss.

By October 1980, 'Prisoner' and another Grundy soap, 'The Restless Years', had pushed the O-TEN Network to the top of the overall ratings, ahead of Seven and Nine, for so long the nemesis of O-TEN. 'The Restless Years' was beating 'CHiPS', and 'Prisoner' trouncing 'Love Boat', another U.S. import.

Late in October, Sheila Florance was Australia's most acclaimed woman TV player, winning a coveted Sammy Award for Best Actress in a Series, an award made even more important because it was judged by her peers – Sammys have the rare distinction of being voted by actors and actresses from both the film and television industries.

Clutching her Sammy the Seal award in one hand and a glass of beer in the other, Sheila still managed to chain-smoke as she told veteran TV reporter Garry Shelley, 'I've never won anything before, although it's my forty-third year in the business. "Prisoner" is my first ongoing TV role. Hell, forget the oldies I played in "Bellbird" and the cop shows, this is my first *real* TV role.'

But she had a sombre warning for her bosses when she revealed how 'Prisoner' was making her physically exhausted. 'I don't know how much longer I can go on like this playing Lizzie. My legs go, so do the arms. I was 64 in July. Sometimes I feel I should just stay at home and look after John and my plants.'.

Early in December a trans-Pacific row erupted when the top-ranking U.S. independent production company Lorimar Pictures (the makers of 'The Waltons', 'Dallas', 'Knots Landing') were accused of pirating ideas from 'Prisoner' for a new series pilot, 'Women In Prison'. Grundy's alleged Lorimar stole parts of the series' scripts. And storyline ideas were indeed the same in several instances. 'Women in Prison' was taped at a Californian penitentiary and starred veteran Ruth Roman as a strong-willed, often arrogant superintendent, and Carol Lynley and Aussie songbird Trish Noble as the principal inmates. Ian Holmes and his senior staff in Sydney got hold of a preview copy of the pilot show when it was being offered around the American networks.

Holmes wouldn't elaborate on the issue, but admitted, 'there has been a bit of a kerfuffle over the matter. I don't know what is going to happen, especially if the show is picked up and goes into series production. However, I can say the "Women in Prison" pilot has caused us considerable concern.' However the concern was short-lived. 'Women in Prison' didn't excite any of the networks and bobbed up as an inferior Movie of the Week while 'Prisoner: Cell Block H' continued to draw American audiences.

9

THE FIRST KEEPERS

Control of Wentworth Detention Centre was supposedly in the hands of Governor Erica Davidson. And from where she sat in her office issuing orders and signing official papers, it seemed she was in total charge. Viewers, though were aware that her well-intentioned authority was confined to signing memos, letters, bulletins and staff orders. Erica (Patsy King) was only a figurehead, albeit for much of her tenure a successful one. Her approach of do-it-by-the-book – or find a better way – bought about some progressive advances. But, in essence, Erica's office and the walled-in prisoners were kept well apart.

Reporters who met Patsy King off the set of 'Prisoner' were in for a pleasant surprise. They'd meet the actress without any trace of Erica Davidson. She would discard the tailored blue suit and neat bun she wore in Wentworth for vibrant coloured dresses and flowing hair. No clipped Governor's voice, either. And Patsy swings her hands and arms around when she talks and gestures. Tidy Governor Erica is very reserved when it comes to body language. 'Yet, she wasn't a stubborn or silly old stick. There was soul, and she did care about regulations and getting the job done with a minimum of fuss,' said Patsy in late 1979.

Fans found it hard to separate Patsy, the actress, from Erica, the character she played so convincingly. Yet, it took only minutes to see Patsy was the antithesis of Erica. 'Actually, I love playing the baddie. I keep pleading with the scriptwriters to give Erica more nasty things to do,' she told *Daily Mirror* reporter, Joanne Sawicki.

She was working for Grundy's on their Sydney series 'Chopper Squad' when they called her in to audition for 'Prisoner'. 'The minute I read the part, I knew it was for me. Of course, it was supposed to be for only sixteen episodes, and while I was happy to have several months' work in Melbourne, where I did all my main stage work with the National Theatre Company, I was thinking about what I'd do after 'Prisoner' finished shooting. Here we are fourteen months later, still in production and the future looks great.'

The second-in-charge at Wentworth, head warder Vera Bennett (Fiona Spence), trod the dimly lit corridors of power with fearful wrath. She possessed hands of steel and a tongue which snapped like a whipcrack. She was sour tempered and had a sadistic streak. Hence the name Vinegar Tits. Vera longed to be Governor of Wentworth. She'd show the world how to run a prison. She thought Erica Davidson too soft, inept at showing the prisoners who was boss and her failure was in not meeting fire with fire.

The prisoners feared Vera Bennett at first and were wary in the extreme, but as the months passed they found chinks even in her fortress-like armour. Yet Vera was no easy target, and her vengeance could be awful. Only a brave heart or a fool took on Vinegar Tits.

Overall, however, the inmates ran Wentworth. Sure, there was a need for compliance to the basic rules of incarceration, but they often rebelled against many of the demands. There were ways and means of controlling the screws, and that meant you could be in charge of the system. As long-term real-life prisoner and series consultant, Sandra Willson, wrote: 'The screws had eight hours a day to come in, adjust and perform. The prisoners have all day and all night to plan their deals. That's why the inmates are always ahead. The screws can't win.' Many real-life prisoners wrote that they had a Vera in their midst. 'Vinegar Tits is here,' several said in their frequent letters. And signs, mainly hand-written, 'Watch Out for Vinegar Tits', started appearing on prison walls and even made it to staff notice-boards.

There was a balance of sensible administration between Erica Davidson and warder Meg Morris (Elspeth Ballantyne). It was a relationship which had its ups and downs, but drew deserved praise from jail officials. Meg possessed an obvious air of authority and had the ideal composure to be a good keeper. She didn't have the sadistic streak of Vera Bennett. Warm-hearted, sympathetic to many of the inmates' problems, but never a tool of their manipulations, she saw her duty as a two-edged sword. Administer the law and play by the rules *à la* Governor Erica Davidson), give the prisoners a chance to redeem themselves, pay their dues and get a good re-start in the outside world. Of course, some inmates saw Meg as a softie, ultimately paying the penalty when they tried to play her for a fool.

The savage losses in Meg's life would have swamped others, but Meg seemed to accept her legacy from being a warder and doing the best she could. In the end, she and the co-operative prisoners reap the benefits of 'playing the game and staying within the limits'.

PRISONER FILE

Name: Sonia Stevens
Actress: Tina Bursill

Sonia Stevens -- later known as 'SS' -- is a tough cookie. A policeman's wife involved in drugs trafficking, prostitution and a standover racket, she wants to be top dog and begins some monumental confrontations with Bea Smith. Totally unpredictable, Sonia would turn on her most devoted allies and fellow inmates breathed a sigh of relief when Sonia made a getaway and was never recaptured.

Norman Yemm appeared as cop Eddie Stevens, Sonia's husband. And his daughter, 17-year-old Jodie Yemm, also appeared as inmate Rosemary Matthews.

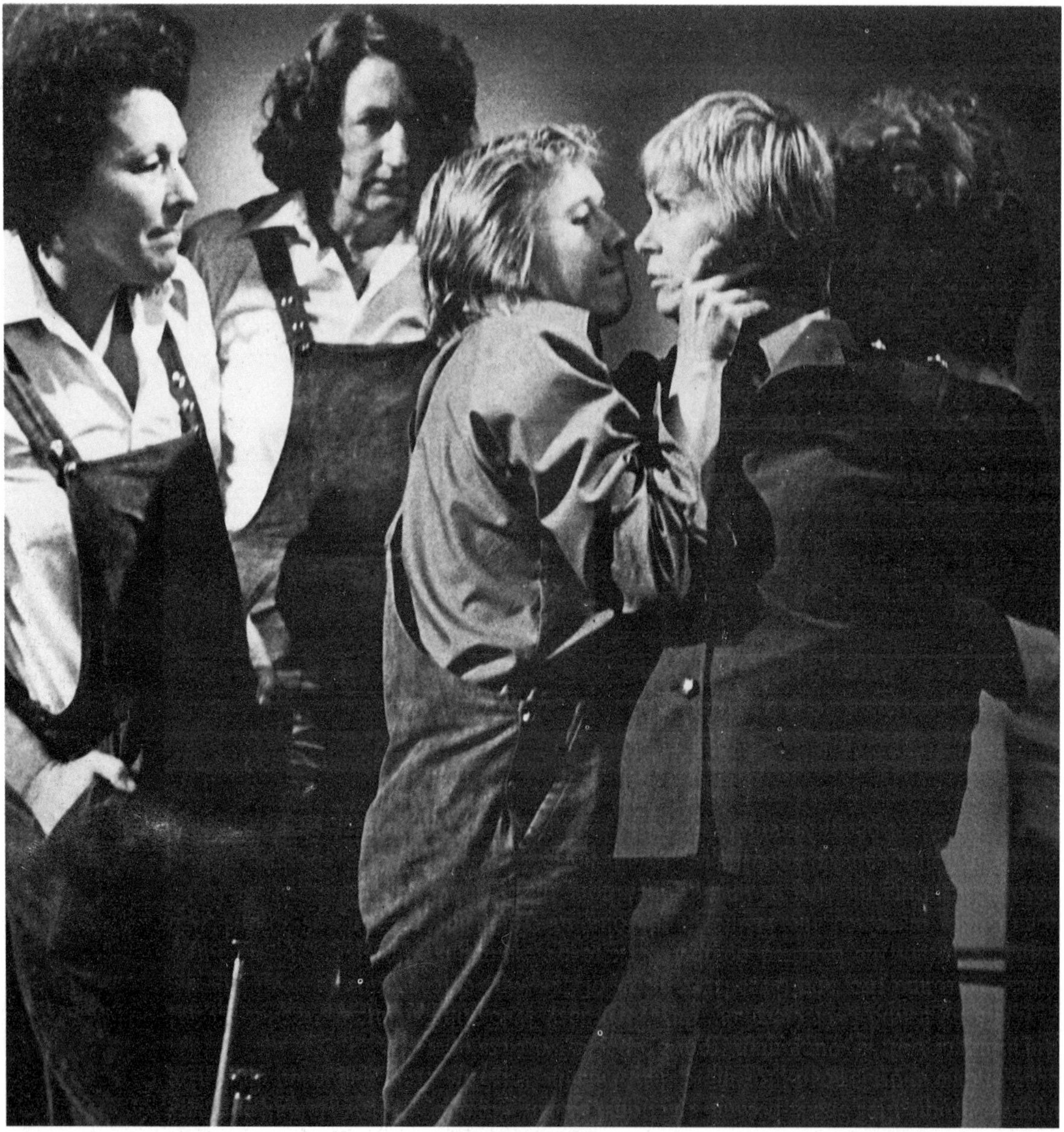

Vintage stuff from Frankie Doyle (Carol Burns) as she tells Officer Meg Morris (Elspeth Ballantyne) what she'd do with her in a dark and lonely cell ... if she got the chance

When 'Prisoner' got underway, Meg was married to jail psychiatrist Bill Jackson (Don Barker), and they had the knack of being able to leave Wentworth behind when going home. There was a 12-year-old son, destined to get a top education and perhaps become a research scientist, a doctor or lawyer. Bill and Meg wouldn't like to see him in the Corrective Services or Prison Department. Enough of that in the family already.

Bill's counselling and trust within the main ranks of prisoners meant he was able to solve a lot of problems often talking common sense to inmates seemingly hell-bent on carnage. On a couple of occasions he actually got through to Franky Doyle in the high moments of a siege or brawl. He couldn't control her, but he could help with his very special kind of calmness.

So, it was tragedy at its blackest when genial Bill was fatally stabbed by inmate Chrissie Latham during a riot at Wentworth. The blade was plunged into his chest and he died in a distraught Meg's arms. It looked like Meg would opt for greener pastures at a smaller prison, or quit the service. But she and Bill were said to have made a pact that if either died then the other would continue to do the work they'd already given so much to over the years.

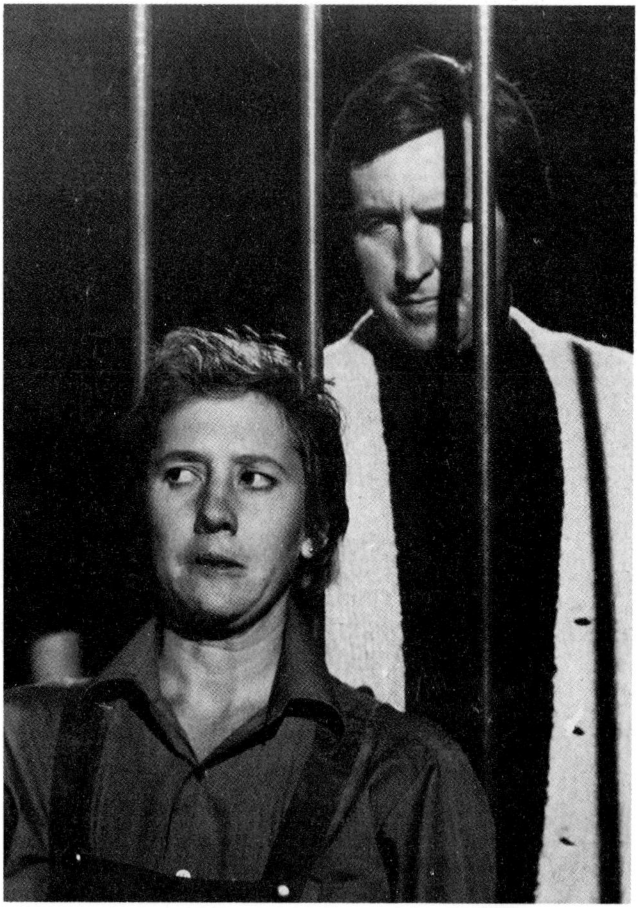

Prison psychologist Bill Jackson (Don Barker) tries to reason with crazed Frankie Doyle (Carol Burns) as a riot erupts at Wentworth. Bill, Meg Morris' husband, is stabbed to death by inmate Chrissie Latham

Gerard Maguire, 35, essayed the first major male keeper role in 'Prisoner'. There had been several men walking around the place, with little to do and less to say, but except for electrician, Eddie Cook (Richard Moir), Doctor Greg Miller (Barry Quin), lawyer, Steve Wilson (Jim Smillie), and prison psychiatrist Bill Jackson, Wentworth was basically an all-female jungle.

Sydney-born Maguire was best known for his array of TV guest roles in many local series. He co-starred as Samuel Firbeck to Oliver Tobias's Luke in 'Luke's Kingdom', the ABC-TV/BBC series (1974-75). He also guested in 'Bellbird', 'Certain Women' and 'The Truckies', and was much in demand for voice-over work on radio and in TV commercials, a busy and lucrative career that continued even after he first trod the jail corridors as Deputy Governor Jim Fletcher.

The authorities had decided things were getting a little unruly at Wentworth and, while basically pleased with Governor Erica Davidson's efforts, wanted some muscle in the front office and among the increasingly militant inmates. The Franky Doyle bullet-ridden road to eternity and the general increase in violence and riots called for a special show of force, even if that meant a man.

Jim Fletcher's suave appearance – he was a neat, moustached, able-bodied officer whose uniform fitted like a glove – at times would serve as a steel-edged reminder of authority and its power to the inmates, but at other times be something of a turn-on for the *femmes*. And debonair Jim knew it, too . . ..

It was no surprise to learn he was a Viet Vet, said to have been on secret missions, one of which saw him save his unit from decimation when he single-handedly wiped out a gun-nest of VC snipers.

Jim Fletcher had been decorated, and looked every inch an officer no matter which uniform he fitted into – something people would notice the moment he came into sight. He had survived the hellish battlefields of Vietnam and returned home to his beautiful young wife Leila. They had two sons, Matthew (10) and David (5). The Fletchers quickly settled into their new life with the Wentworth appointment. It was obvious Jim's next posting would be as Superintendent or even Governor of either Wentworth, or a bigger prison.

Fletcher's arrival as second-in-command at Wentworth irked Vera Bennett. She'd

PRISONER FILE

Name: Gloria Marshall

Actress: Totty Goldsmith

Glamorous trouble-maker Gloria Marshall was played by the 20-year-old niece of Olivia Newton-John, Totty Goldsmith. Her parents are Rona Newton-John and Brian Goldsmith, founders of the highly successful Melbourne nightclub, Underground.

been hopeful when officialdom began questioning Erica Davidson's effectiveness as Governor. For a while it looked like Vera might get the top job by default. However, Fletcher's muscle and past record as a strict but well intentioned keeper triumphed, if in fact the penal bosses had ever actually considered the rival merits of the two officers. Maybe all that was only in Vera's mind?

Still, behind all the stories of Vietnam bravery and the ability to administer regulations under pressure, Jim Fletcher arrived at Wentworth with a secret that could cost him his job, even his life. He had been relieved of his duties at his most recent posting, a renowned tough male prison, because of his anti-violence stand, a reaction against Vietnam genocide.

In true 'Prisoner' fashion, Vietnam follows Jim Fletcher to his new domain in Wentworth when unit buddy Geoff Butler (played by Ray Meagher, later to become Summer Bay kingpin Alf Stewart in 'Home and Away') decides to pay a visit. It doesn't take Geoff long to realise Jim is a changed man from their Vietnam days, but Geoff brightens up when he meets and starts dating a somewhat nervous Meg Morris (she has always used her maiden name when working in the prison). It is obvious Meg is still trying to overcome the horror and ordeal of seeing her husband murdered in the jail riot. But she is pleased, that a man is showing special interest.

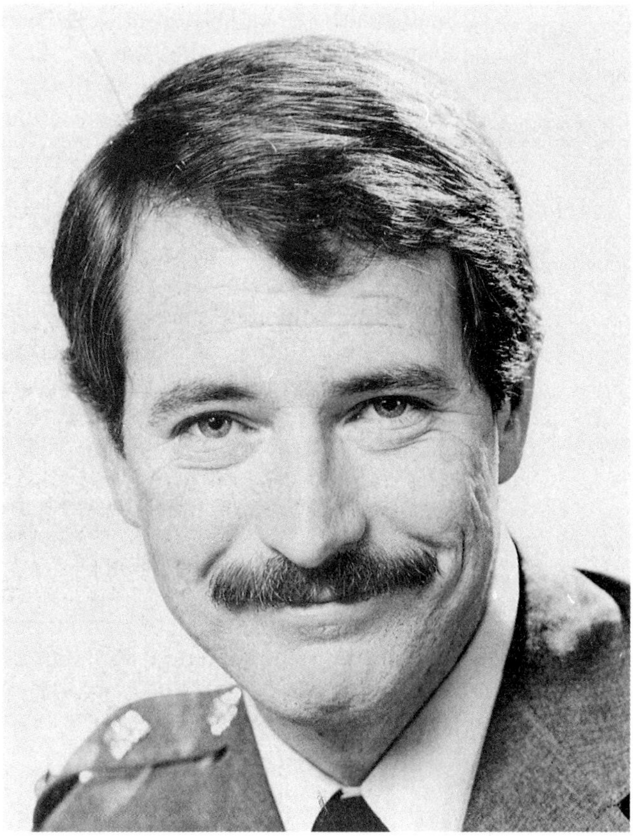

Wentworth Deputy Governor Jim Fletcher (Gerard Maguire), brought in as up-front muscle for Wentworth, lost his wife and two kids to a demented Vietnam buddy's parcel bomb

Things go badly wrong with the budding romance. Geoff pushes too hard with a wary Meg and assaults her. Finding himself in court with Jim Fletcher a witness against him, Butler swears horrific revenge. Calling on his Viet skills, a demonic Geoff builds a parcel bomb and sends it to Jim. The deadly package ends up in a spine-tingling tug-of-war between young Matthew and David Fletcher and, as their mum Leila intervenes, the bomb explodes, killing all three.

Shocked viewers would later rate the bomb deaths as the most traumatic Wentworth event since Franky Doyle's death.

Joyce Barry (a fine, understated role by Joy Westmore) was 'the background warder' in the early phases of 'Prisoner' but, as the series began to swing more of the jailers' lives into full view, Joyce's personal and home problems would be played out, and she soon became much more interesting to viewers. She'd even find a lover.

Judith McGrath also began in the background as Officer Colleen Powell. Once her personal trials and tribulations were unveiled viewers realised a second time that there was a lot more to the women in uniform than they had been led to believe.

Looking back through those 1979-80 episodes of 'Prisoner', the emphasis on characters and storylines was thrust firmly in the direction of inmates Franky Doyle and Bea Smith. Jailers Erica Davidson, Vera Bennett and Meg Morris suffered somewhat from storyline neglect, but this was rectified when John McRae took over from initial producer Ian Bradley. Most of the major cast changes in the next two seasons of 'Prisoner' would be on the right side of the law, among the keepers of the inmates. More and more was happening to the jailers, particularly in their private lives.

The two 'background' officers Joyce Barry (Joy Westmore) and Colleen Powell (Judith McGrath) were being given heavier workloads, although the emphasis was still on Governor Erica Davidson (Patsy King) and Warders Vera Bennett (Fiona Spence) and Meg Morris (Elspeth Ballantyne). The Deputy Governor Jim Fletcher (Gerard Maguire) was by now a short-term proposition.

As Pixie Mason (Judy McBurney) had brought some fun and levity to Wentworth's cell-block, it seemed a good idea to inject some humour into the jailers' domain. A male stripper was smuggled in to a forty-fourth birthday party for Bea Smith, causing

PRISONER FILE

Name: Angela Adams

Actress: Kylie Foster

Angela is a spoilt girl who rebels against her parents and burns down their house -- with them in it, described by actress Kylie Foster as 'a thoroughly rotten, nasty and real bad seed'.

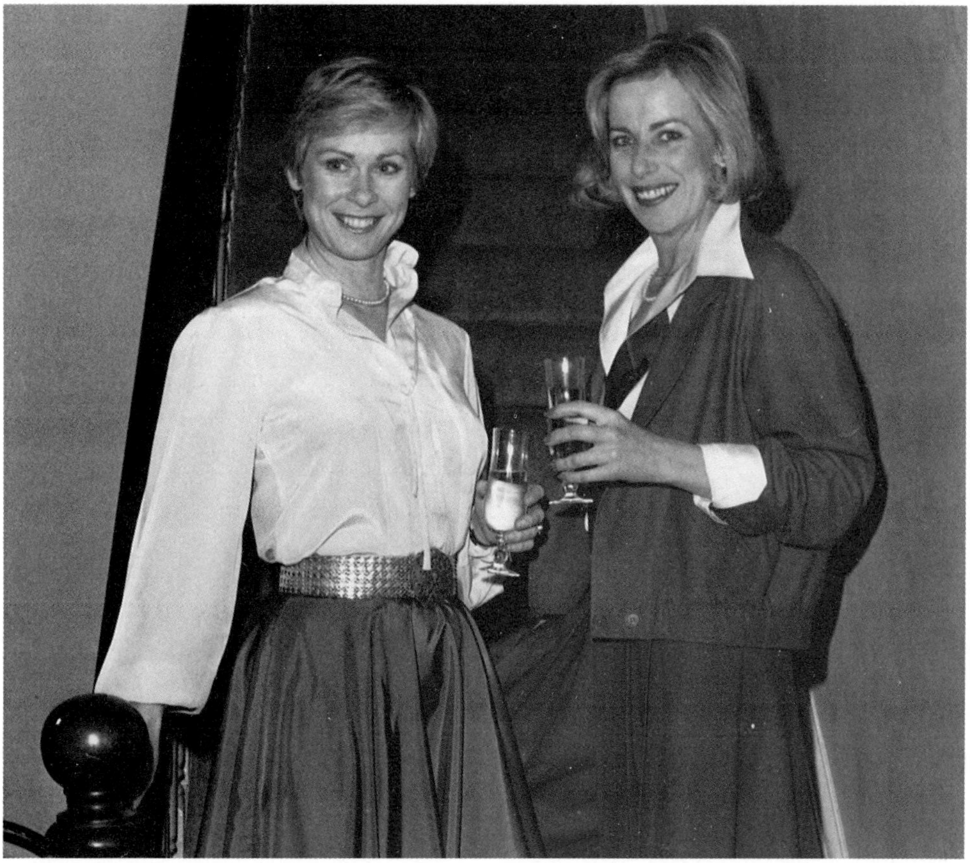

Patsy King made it to the 300th episode party for 'Prisoner' to renew acquaintance with her former cast colleagues. No sign of Governor Erica Ferguson, and Elspeth Ballantyne was far removed from warder Meg Morris' usual uniform. *(Solo Syndication)*

Governor Davidson some red-faced moments. She'd okayed the party for Queen Bea – 'The women need to have fun from time to time' – but *not* a stripper. The inmates had organised a special diversion to keep the guards busy, and their plan almost worked. In the end, after officialdom had been placated, everyone, including the stripper and the Governor had a few laughs.

It was good to see Erica having a laugh, even at her own expense. She'd been suspended pending an inquiry into her association with a clothing factory operated by Andrew Reynolds (John Lee), which was used as work-experience for a group of prisoners. Following a highly volatile report from Vera Bennett, Erica faced allegations that she had had an illicit affair with Reynolds (actually it was a perfectly natural

SONG OF THE NIGHT

In mid-May 1989, a worldwide search began for Sixties and Seventies star Lynne Hamilton, singer of 'On the Inside', the haunting theme song for the closing credits of 'Prisoner: Cell Block H'.

'On the Inside' was climbing the British charts as the series started grabbing millions of regular viewers on the ITV Network. Explained Ray Levy, the A1 Pop Record Company managing director in London, 'On instinct we released the "Prisoner" theme song single earlier than planned. It started to do very well, but we couldn't find Lynne to help with the promotion. Many people said she was no longer in the business and had retired to be an anonymous housewife.'

In fact, Lynne was basking in the sunshine of the Gold Coast near Brisbane, Queensland, when her family learned the London company was looking for the Lancashire-born singer. 'It was like history repeating itself,' said Lynne. ' "On the Inside" shot to number one in the Australian charts ten years ago when "Prisoner" was first aired, and now it's hurtling up the charts in the U.K.' (It eventually reached number four.)

Lynne had already been a successful entertainer in the U.K. and Europe, but was an unknown singer in Australia when asked to record 'On the Inside', written by one of Australia's best known country singer-composers Allan Caswell (Oz Country Singer of the Year, 1988). The Grundy Organization had gone to the RCA company and asked for an unknown singer to record the theme song.

'They chose me, the unknown,' quips Lynne, now 40.

Lynne had started singing at the age of 15 in England with a teen backing group The Desperadoes, working and touring with outfits like The Who, the Animals and Freddy and the Dreamers. Then came a four-year stint in a duo, The Caravelles, touring Europe and the U.K. before splitting up. 'My musical ideas were developing, changing. I wanted to keep up with the competition. The other girl didn't agree.'

Lynne decided to try her luck away from the demanding routine of day and night travelling to gigs all over Europe, and headed Down Under to the sunshine and rolling golden beaches of the Gold Coast. 'I wasn't quite 20, had saved $30,000 (£13,760), which was a lot of money in 1971. So, I brought out my mum and two sisters and decided to become my own self-made businesswoman. First I ran a car rental agency, then a lingerie shop, and finally a restaurant. none of them really worked out.

'I ran into an old friend, George Dilanian. He couldn't believe I had stopped singing and took over my management. Then came the RCA call to record "On the Inside". I had an agent, John Hansen, and things looked good when the song became a megahit in Australia. It sold more than 80,000 copies. I was then living in the Sydney suburb of Killarney Heights to be closer to the hub of the club scene.

'I did a lot of gigs, but the second hit wasn't there, so I moved to the States for three years. Yes, I knew the series was a big hit there but Pattie Page had recorded a slow country ballad of "On the Inside". I didn't have a deal for an American release or residuals, but writer Allan Caswell did. I decided long ago it's no use crying over spilt milk.'

The timing of Lynne Hamilton's recall to triumph in England couldn't have been better – record producer Mike Howells said she was in for 'a heap of royalties' – as Lynne had just completed a new album in Los Angeles. The mother of two daughters made sure she went to Chorley, Lancashire, for a poignant reunion with her bricklayer dad Reg. An unashamed 'Prisoner' addict, he is, too.

grown-up relationship). Vera also claimed Erica had used the factory to further her own financial ends. It took the hierarchy weeks to decide Erica was innocent of the accusations.

Twice, when under tremendous pressure, Erica had resigned, but was talked into returning. She also withstood some heavy flak about supposed preferential treatment of a niece sent to Wentworth on drug-related charges. As viewers knew, Erica may have been a little soft in some areas, but she didn't do anyone any favours.

No sooner had it been announced that Gerard Maguire was quitting the show, a new female warder, Christine Simmons, was checking the cells at Wentworth. A NIDA graduate of 1970, Kate Sheil was a seasoned actress with ample stage and TV credits ('Bellamy', 'Cop Shop') and had been in a Bruce Beresford movie, *Puberty Blues* (1978). Her style of operation was by the book and, if you behaved yourself, life would be a lot easier day and night.

Sydney actor Wayne Jarratt, 25, was the second of the full-time male jailers at Wentworth, a dark-haired, hard-working, disciplined player who relished being in his first major TV role. As the cheeky Steve Fawkner, he 'was able to get his teeth into an interesting character role, a ladies' man, with a tendency to break prison rules', said the amiable Jarratt in his first major interview.

Jarratt told *Melbourne Herald* writer Yasmine Willan his character of Fawkner 'was a little weak at times, but it was a likeable weakness, he wasn't a wimp. Getting involved with a female prisoner was a no-no, for a male guard, but my guy does just that. He romances a really heavy number in former underworld moll Sandy Edwards. Alas, she leaves the scene during an escape in which she gets into a garbage truck unaware the compaction unit is about to be used. Grim stuff, but real.'

Just as 'Prisoner's' new producer John McRae took over the reins and announced a build-up in cast numbers, Vinegar Tits Bennett was about to be written out of the show. Fans were upset and swags of protesting mail arrived at the studio. The switchboard took more than 100 calls asking Fiona to reconsider her decision. 'Stay a little longer,' the fans pleaded. They'd grown attached to the imposing character who meted out her own kind of justice as she patrolled the Wentworth corridors.

Even one Sydney scribe admitted he would miss her greatly. 'Vera would be completely at home striding through the grounds of Belsen and Auschwitz concentration camps. She does it all so well.'

But there was no keeping Wentworth's resident ogress in uniform. 'I loved playing Vera,' said Fiona Spence. 'But it was time to wash that dame right out of my hair.'

Working out her final weeks, Fiona Spence started to pay particular attention to Vera Bennett's hair-style and lipstick. A new male guard was on the scene – Brendan Wilson (played by former 'Bellbird' regular Brian Hannan, now a very successful voice-over and TV comercials actor) – and he starts to fancy Vera. It is all because of a bet he had with a mate, but in the process he genuinely falls for Vera. Viewers could hardly wait to see how Vinegar Tits handled the kissin' and the cuddlin'.

Fiona Spence was tearful as she did the round of farewells. The Wentworth set had been her home for more than two years. 'We all knew we'd miss her,' said Val Lehman. 'Forget the character, Fi was fun to work with. No one remembers lines like she does. She's off home to sleep this party off, and we'll be back tomorrow with hangovers. That's more like a parting gift from old Vinegar Tits.'

Val herself, along with Colette Mann and Gerard Maguire, was about to take a break to shoot the movie *Kitty and the Bagman*. So, much of the script was now being thrown at the female jailers. Quipped Colette: 'About time Elspeth, Judy, Joy and Erica got some homework. Happy script-reading, girls.'

10

THE WINNING OF AMERICA

'Prisoner' was twenty-nine episodes down the track in Australia when it was first screened in the United States, but its exposure to the world's biggest potential market in the western world meant some changes at home. A changed name and a closer look at some of the new and incoming prisoners became necessary, as well as the introduction of further males, but not on a token basis.

Grundy's realised they had tapped into a goldmine previously denied to the very parochial Australian drama industry – and this was the first major Grundy foray into the international market at near top-level. The rewards from these first 'Prisoner' sales wouldn't be big but beyond the initial Los Angeles screening lay the possibility of lucrative additional markets in other major cities and the golden chance to have considerable regular money coming back to the home coffers in Los Angeles and Sydney.

'Prisoner' premièred on KTLA-5, Los Angeles, on 8 August 1979. The station was the biggest of the city's independent outfits, but usually had to be content as number four on the ratings lists behind the mammoth ABC, CBS and NBC conglomerates and their national networks. Still, it had a reputation for taking shots at the big boys.

KTLA-5 bosses and programmers first saw the Oz show at a sales convention in Las Vegas in April, 1979, but it took three months of trans-Pacific negotiations between Los Angeles and Sydney executives to finalise the precedent-making deal. The Yanks made an immediate and major change – the show was re-titled 'Prisoner: Cell Block H'. The American programmers claimed they didn't want their latest acquisition to be confused with the popular U.K. series 'The Prisoner', starring Patrick McGoohan, a worldwide hit in the Sixties, and in its umpteenth repeat in several U.S. markets. And the U.K. producers of the original 'Prisoner' were geared to sue the new series if the title was used Stateside.

Grundy staff in Australia say there was no pressure to make blatant changes in 'Prisoner' to satisfy any special demands from KTLA-5, although 'certain ideas and suggestions were floated in from time to time'. In many U.S. areas the show was seen in a half-hour format five days or nights a week rather than as a one-hour series. The violence, swearing or sex elements were toned down in re-edited episodes freighted to

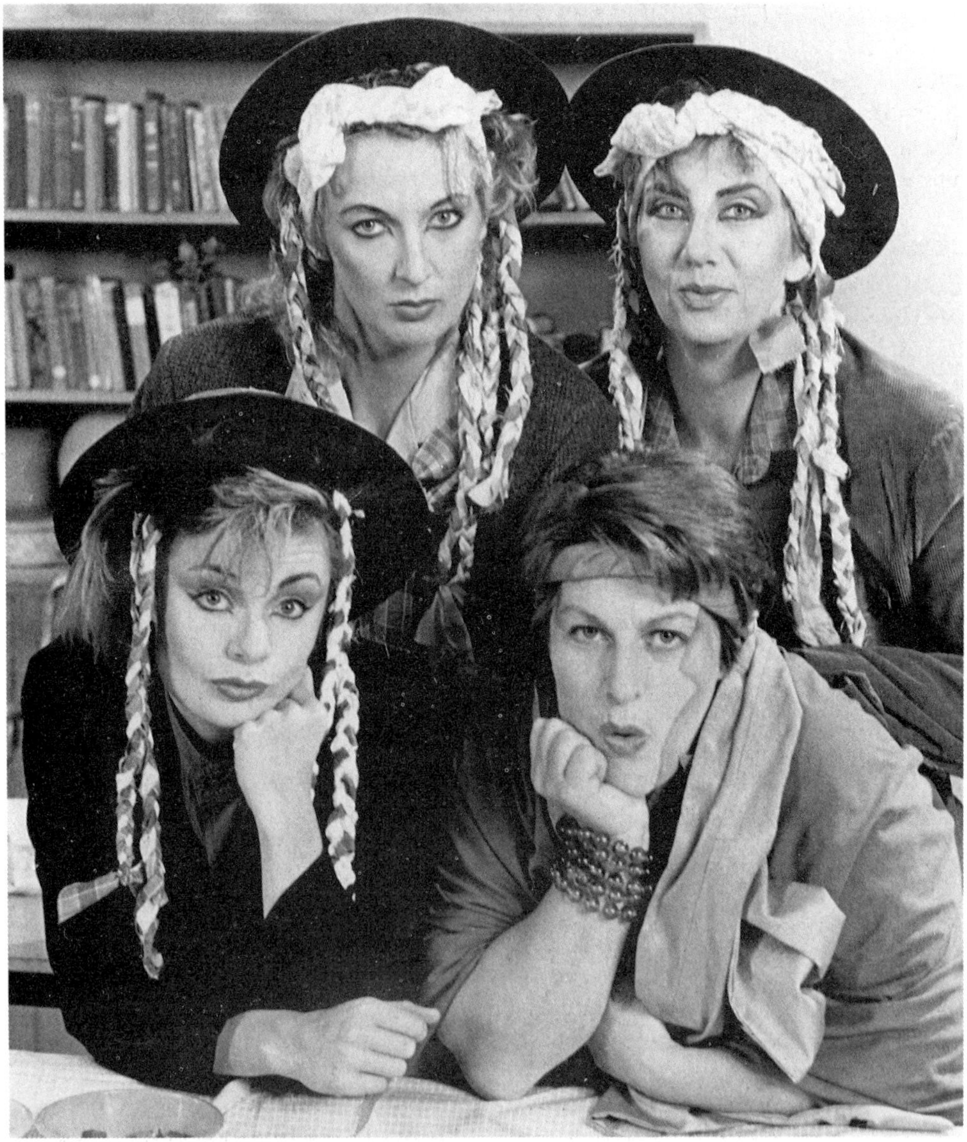

It's Boy George dress-up time when Bobbie Mitchell's pals celebrate her impending release. *Back*: Rita Connors (Glenda Linscott), Alice Watkins (Lois Collinder). *Front*: Lorelei Wilkinson (Paula Duncan) and Merle Jones (Rosanne Hull-Brown)

Los Angeles. And the Aussies were told to minimise ocker slang words.

Grundy's could see an expanding market in the States and elsewhere (there were nibbles from Canada, England and New Zealand), so anything that could boost potential sales got a good hearing from the producers. But a plan to import several 'name' American actresses for guest roles was turned down early on because of the immediate and expected reaction from the Actors' Equity union and the cast itself.

While viewers in California switched on to 'Prisoner: Cell Block H' in droves, the reviewers and critics generally blasted the inmates of Wentworth, though some had the good sense (or took an each-way bet) to suggest the show could be 'contagious or addictive'.

KTLA-5 made no bones about why it was screening 'Prisoner'. Said a spokesman

PRISONER FILE

Name: Alice 'Lurch' Watkins

Actress: Lois Collinder

5 ft 10 ins Lois Collinder caught the attention of the 'Prisoner' casting office when she played in 'Carson's Law'. Signed up as 'a heavy -- we'll keep you in the background', this was just what happened for about 19 months. She was a mystery all this time, acting as a stooge or bodyguard for the top dogs in Wentworth, until she was finally given a name -- Alice Watkins. Inside for a seven year stretch, Alice had been a country girl looking for kicks when she joined up with a lethal gang who carried out armed robberies. In a bungled job, gangly Alice is abandoned and the rest of the gang speed off into the night, leaving her to take the rap.

Lois had been a dancer before joining 'Prisoner'. The nickname 'Lurch' came when director Kendal Flanagan started confusing the names of the actresses after a long day. Lois recalls: 'Kendal was calling out Lois, Lou, Alice, Rita, Glenda.

'Out of earshot he referred to me as Lurch -- like the towering butler in ''The Addams Family''. The name stuck and got picked up by the writers.'

Lurch may be a late developer in the series, but she is in the forefront of the action when Lou Kelly bursts out of prison and goes on the rampage. She reaches Lurch's family home and murders both her mother (Moira Clau) and adored brother (Steve Millichamp). The grieving Lurch tries to commit suicide but survives. Only days later, she smuggles in a stash of cocaine by remote control car. When Steve Ryan (Peter Hayes) finds it, Lurch catches him and knocks him out. Life is never dull around Lurch . . .

'We want to hook adult viewers seeking relief from the early evening pap on other stations.'

The *Los Angeles Times* critic Howard Rosenberg wrote: 'Whatever else, "Prisoner" isn't pap. Don't expect subtlety. Viewers in search of ferocity can count on a hanging, knifing, shooting, burning and violent furniture-throwing rage. "Prisoner" is strictly capital punishment if you're not sweet on action-melodrama that slides off on to the soft shoulders of soap opera. As seen here, prison life never seems quite as drab as it should be. Yet "Prisoner" may be the kind of silly stuff that can grow on you if you don't quickly flick it away.'

Frank Torrez, of the *Los Angeles Examiner,* wrote: 'This sudsy and very depressing look at women in prison is not going to be mistaken for masterpiece theatre. Admittedly, it's a little tougher and more depressing – if that's possible – than American soaps, but all the basic ingredients are there – sex, broken marriages, several subplots, frequent confrontations, stereotyped characters and lots of crying.'

Charles Parker, of the *Valley News,* which has a big circulation in Hollywood and the San Fernando Valley, where much of the tinsel town workforce lives, saw the show as a breakthrough. 'It is an experiment that could fizzle like a wet firecracker or explode like a stick of dynamite. The station is daring to put on a most adult programme in the sacrosanct so-called family hour.'

Variety, the showbiz bible, was high in praise for the Wentworth girls. 'A gritty and gripping dramatic series . . . the yarn has a lot sharper focus than would be likely in a U.S. production.'

Yet the *Hollywood Reporter* slammed the show. 'So soapsy and trite, with on-the-sleeve acting almost visible. But the theme of dames in prison undoubtedly will hook its audience seeking full-throttle emoting'.

The National Organisation for Women (NOW) objected to 'Prisoner's 'excessive violence and depiction of women in general.'

About forty-five members of Hollywood's Gay Community assembled to picket the KTLA-5 offices after 'Prisoner's' first screening. They were upset about the way in which Franky Doyle was portrayed. Protestors carried placards reading FREE FRANKY

PRISONER FILE

Name: Meryl King
Actress: Marilyn Maguire

24-year-old Meryl is the answer to Sonia Stevens's (Tina Bursill) blues when she comes to share her cell. She is given free rein for high drama. 'Meryl's a prostitute and drug addict going nowhere but an early grave,' said actress Marilyn. 'She has news for Sonia about her policeman husband, but Meryl's destined for a quick come-uppance.'

PRISONER FILE

Name: Reb Keane

Actress: Janet Andrewartha

19-year-old James Dean freak, Reb, is sentenced to seven years for armed robbery. Her good looks hide an evil mind and she soon starts a drugs racket with one of her new buyers nearly dying after being slipped cocaine disguised in a biscuit. Later in the series, she sends a powerful letter to the Governor full of accusations about the Freak. Even when Keane's lies are exposed, the authorities decide that Ferguson must go.

DOYLE, 'PRISONER' IS A CRIME AGAINST LESBIANS and LESBIANS DEMAND BETTER MEDIA IMAGES. The protestors demanded the show be taken off immediately, or each episode be followed by a talk from a member of their community. (CBS, which was suffering most among the networks as 'Prisoner' attracted a regular 2,000,000 viewers, ran prime-time news footage of the gay picket, which gave KTLA-5 an unexpected promotional bonus.)

Only ABC's fairy-floss floozies 'Charlie's Angels' could out-rate Franky, Bea, Lizzie and Co. in the Wednesday 8 p.m. timeslot. KTLA-5 had the second top show among 65 programmes transmitted prime-time on Wednesday nights by the eleven Los Angeles stations. It promptly ordered another twenty-six episodes.

KTLA executive Mary Barron said L.A. people were tuning into 'Prisoner' every week because 'it is so different and it grows on you'. The big networks were caught napping and a beleaguered CBS saw four of their costly new series go down the proverbial gurgler – 'Dorothy', 'Hanging In', 'Struck by Lightning' and 'The Last Resort' (no connection with the equally disastrous Oz ABC-TV series of the same name) – cancelled as 'Prisoner' swamped them.

Grundy's president Ian Holmes admitted there had been some apprehension in America about the parochial nature of the series, including the accents. 'But the ratings and audience response have dispelled any doubts and there have been no problems understanding the accents.'

Then late in 1979 'Prisoner' was sold to Global TV Network, in Toronto, Canada, and underwent another name-change, airing as 'Caged Women'.

The continuing success of 'Prisoner' over-shadowed a Grundy corporate milestone. Supremo Reg Grundy stepped down as president of the group, but still retained his role as chairman, concentrating his activities in the Los Angeles office, which was producing game shows for the American market. He was delighted about the success of 'Prisoner', and gave much of the business credit to Ian Holmes, who was named the new president.

Early in 1980 Grundy's general manager John Fowler reported 'Prisoner' had been sold for syndication to eight other U.S. cities – New York, Chicago, San Diego, Denver, St. Louis, Tampa, Minneapolis and Albuquerque. No figures were mentioned, but within weeks the Sydney press was confirming stories that the initial fourteen episodes to KTLA-5 had netted U.S. $50,000 (£24,000). Later, substantially higher rates were negotiated when the show scored big in the ratings across the States and looked like running for years.

The first major scene of triumph was New York, where 'Prisoner' knocked off the perennial late-night winner 'Johnny Carson's Tonight Show' and re-runs of the legendary 'M*A*S*H'. Another five million people were already watching the girls from Wentworth. Elsewhere, 'watch it and you're hooked' seemed the vogue as Stateside audiences reached an estimated 20 million.

Then came what cast members back home considered the ultimate compliment – the top American satirical comedy show 'Saturday Night Live' did a special skit on 'Prisoner' titled 'Debs Behind Bars' Val Lehman recalls. 'They sent us a copy and it was a real hoot.'

Way up in Alaska, 'Prisoner' was putting plenty of heat into the far northern chill. *Anchorage Times* television critic, Ron Hendren, welcomed the arrival of the show. 'Things are bursting out Down Under. Lately they've been coming up with some innovative programmes and "Prisoner" is one of the best. In an era when American television seems to be growing more and more dependent on spin-offs of proven sitcoms, this dramatic offering from Australia is a welcome change of pace.'

But it wasn't all approbation.

The influential mass-circulation *TV Guide* hammered the show mercilessly: 'A murderer, a convicted prostitute who has an affair with an electrician, an ugly lesbian, a former cook who poisoned her employers and a kidnapper who swears she didn't try to bury an infant alive – these are some of the charmers in "Prisoner: Cell Block H", a sleazy soap-opera produced in Australia. It's hard enough to believe that adult viewers want a series that panders to the shabbiest, most sadistic tastes. It is much harder – in fact, it's sickening to think that in several large cities some stations don't mind if the kids watch, too.

'The series was intended by its syndicator for late-night viewing. But in Minneapolis, this sordid trash is served up to viewers at 6.30 p.m. – to be enjoyed along with dinner, no doubt. In Los Angeles, it's shown at 8 p.m., presumably on one station's theory that the folks in L.A. want to ooze into their serious viewing with a dose of Slime Time.

'Philadelphia, the City of Brotherly Love, is the worst offender of all. There, "Prisoner" comes on at 5 p.m., when even the youngest kids can see it before dinner, thus losing their appetites but gaining a whole new appreciation of life in the gutter.'

Nevertheless, cast members in Melbourne were getting calls from American viewers. The overseas mail poured in. In one week mid-1980, O-TEN at Nunawading received twenty-four American calls, most wanting to talk to Lizzie or Bea, and in the same period about 1,200 U.S.A. letters were passed out to Wentworth inmates – on top of more than 3,000 local letters. A former station telephonist tells of one persistent lady from San Diego who would call in vain twice a week to try and find out what was happening in the episodes ahead. She gave up after nearly four weeks. New Yorkers and Californians were spotted wearing 'I Love Lizzie' T-shirts, which was a great tonic for Sheila Florance. By late-1980 'Prisoner' was on thirty-eight stations across America.

The cult following of 'Prisoner' fascinated a Los Angeles-based Australian producer and three years later she would be producing the show. Sue Masters now one of Australia's top rated TV producers (her latest work is the ABC-TV/BBC mini-series 'The Paper Man', shot in Sydney and London with an international cast – Oliver Tobias, John Bach, Peta Toppano, Rebecca Gilling, Olivia Hamnett and Jonathon Hyde) recalls how she got hooked. 'It had an extraordinary following in San Francisco. People used to dress up in clothes like the inmates wore on "Prisoner", then get together at each other's houses to watch it on air.'

Masters had written scripts for shows like 'Barney Miller', 'Love Boat' and 'Rhoda' and produced variety shows for cable TV. She even did a stint as creative development director for Burt Reynolds' television company. Masters told *Daily Mirror* writer Liz Porter: 'All this mild fantasy island stuff, then one night I tuned into "Prisoner". I liked it immediately because it was gutsy, different. And I thought at the time if I ever went back home, what a buzz it would be to work on the show one day.'

Returning home a year later, Masters went to work for Grundy's on their top-rating and long-running 'The Young Doctors'. A year later she was switched to 'Prisoner' as producer to replace exiting Phil East (co-opted to another Grundy soap, 'Neighbours').

'Prisoner's' success obviously helped other Oz shows seeking a place in the foreign markets. Bob Crystal, head of the West Coast office of Reg Grundy Productions, believes it paved the way for major money buys of the mini-series 'Against the Wind' (Seven Network) and 'The Sullivans' (Nine). 'The Sullivans', from the rival Crawford outfit, was sold to Los Angeles for $600,000 (£285,000). No figures have been publicly released on 'Prisoner's eventual returns from the States, but industry observers believe it was in excess of $4.2-million (£2,000,000).

It was May 1981, before the next international sale of 'Prisoner' – New Zealand TV1 bought the show at an undisclosed price and promptly screened it twice a week at 2.30 in the afternoons.

It would be nearly nine years before England would be the next big success story for the Wentworth girls, surprisingly third in line on a wave that was led by two Johnny-come-lately teen shows 'Neighbours' and 'Home And Away' though neither of these major Oz and U.K. hits has been seen in the United States.

REAL LIFE CATCHES UP

When Grundy's introduced former 'Sullivans' star Vivien Gray into 'Prisoner' as husband-poisoner Edna Pearson, they weren't prepared for the possibility of a writ from a woman in South Australia who in 1982 successfully appealed against a conviction for attempting to poison her husband. But Mrs Emily Gertrude Phyllis Perry went public claiming the seven episodes in which the Pearson character appeared had defamed her.

Mrs Perry was the central figure in a sensational 72-day trial in 1981 which revolved around Crown allegations that she had tried to kill her husband by putting small doses of arsenic in his food. Her husband Kenneth Warwick Henry Perry steadfastly maintained his wife's innocence throughout the trial. Mrs. Perry was sentenced to fifteen years in jail, but was freed after her conviction was quashed by the High Court in 1982. The Government decided against a retrial.

'I have no doubts that the general storyline of Ms Pearson was based on evidence I gave during my trial,' Mrs Perry claimed on a radio chat show when she announced she was considering suing Grundy's for defamation. Mrs Perry said since making contact with Grundy's they had edited out all the scenes involving Mrs Pearson for "Prisoner" episodes airing in Adelaide to spare me any further embarrassment'.

Grundy's told Mrs Perry their Mrs Pearson character was based on the case of a woman jailed in 1953 for the poisoning of her husband. Mrs Perry did not take the matter to court after Grundy's published announcements in capital city daily newspapers stating that the 'Prisoner' story concerning the Mrs Pearson character was in no way connected with Mrs Perry's case.

11

ENTER THE FREAK

The 1982 Australian Christmas-New Year vacation over, 'Prisoner' was soon back before the cameras and playing with fire in an episode when Lizzie Birdsworth's inspiration, a moonshining experiment within the walls of Wentworth Jail, went wrong. Unsuspecting guard Steve Fawkner unwittingly makes a major contribution to the blaze and is almost killed after an explosion threatens to burn down the prison. Lizzie's idea for the illicit stills works so well there is soon a storage problem. So the inmates fill the nearest fire-extinguishers with the brew, giving easy access on those many cold, lonely nights.

When the screws do a sudden search for a secret letter, Doreen Anderson sets fire to a mattress as a diversion. Fawkner arrives to fight the cell fire with a blanket, but has to resort to the nearest extinguisher. He is unaware it is full of pure alcohol. The subsequent explosion hurls him across the room, badly burning his legs. Other staff and firemen put out the blaze.

When Grundy's were told Patsy King was thinking of leaving the show some major recruiting got underway – and the biggest impact on the show since Franky Doyle, Bea Smith and Lizzie Birdsworth was about to happen.

Enter the Freak! Warder Joan Ferguson, a malevolent force of terrifying moods and evil desires.

Maggie Kirkpatrick, 40, was perfect as Ferguson. A well-established theatre actress with a solid sprinkling of TV and movie credits ('The John Denver Special', 'Jonah', 'The Oracle', 'Spring and Fall'; and on the big screen *F. J. Holden, The Getting of Wisdom, The Night of the Prowler* and *The Pirate Movie*) she was born in Albury, the New South Wales border town.

In lean times before 'Prisoner', Maggie often worked part time pulling beers at the Strand Hotel in William Street, Sydney, a well-known hangout for the acting fraternity. But all that changed in June of 1982 when Maggie donned the jail uniform of Warder Joan Ferguson, flexed her black-gloved hands and strode the corridors of Wentworth. She was a stand-out from her very first entrance.

If Franky Doyle had electrified 'Prisoner' fans, Lizzie Birdsworth endeared herself to all and Bea Smith tugged at their heart-strings, Ferguson would rip them apart. Her arrival as a sensational new character was said by many industry insiders to have saved 'Prisoner', or at least given it a new lease of life.

This jailer knew all the tricks, had conquered the toughest inmates in other prisons, and usually knew in advance just what the prisoners were planning. Here was someone in uniform just as corrupt or cruel as the worst of the inmates, but she was on the other side of the bars, legally administering her own very special kind of justice. Wentworth inmates quickly learned to avoid the wrath of the Freak. She was in her own adult Disneyland, a world of bizarre and sadistic rituals.

The durable Chrissie Latham (Amanda Muggleton) was back in Wentworth about the time Ferguson signed on – and Chrissie knew from her outside sources the Freak's dark secret of an affair with another female guard in a Queensland jail. Ferguson had quit her previous post rather than endure the torture of her ex-lover's indifference or risk subjection to an official investigation. Latham moves in on Ferguson to take advantage of the warder's offbeat sexual preferences. Latham lets it be known she will seduce the Freak. But her plan backfires and life behind bars becomes tougher for Chrissie instead of more tender.

And the first of the momentous Freak v. Bea Smith duels begins. 'I often wondered if I had gone in too fast and too heavy with Ferguson,' said Maggie Kirkpatrick after a fortnight in the demanding role. 'It's hard to stand back and evaluate your own work when you're in so many scenes. You just wander home after taping and collapse into bed each night, check lines for the next day, then sleep, get up and do it all again. Ferguson is a tough role. So much of her is based on the physical side. But what a role! Any actress would kill to play Fergie!'

Later that year, Sue Masters arrived to produce 'Prisoner'. Her wish in San Francisco to one day work on the cult show had come true for the Australian globe-trotter. 'Now that Bea has left we'll be trying to get a more interesting mix of prisoners. The violence will be toned down, and there'll be more lightness,' said Sue.

That didn't apply to Joan Ferguson. She got tougher and more dangerous. The

PRISONER FILE

Name: Hannah Geldsmidt

Actress: Agnieszka Perpeczko

Hannah is a German Jew, haunted by the spectre of a Nazi concentration camp where she lived as a baby. She finds herself in jail when she assaults a man who resembles the SS officer of her nightmares. Later, they discover she is an illegal immigrant so she faces deportation and persecution back home.

A real-life drama was played out behind the scenes when Polish actress Agnieszka Perpeczko, 40, came to visit her brother in 1981. She had stayed on but her husband was still in Poland. 'I saw what a beautiful country it was and decided I wanted to stay.' Her husband of 19 years, Marek, did eventually get a passport and flew out to meet her.

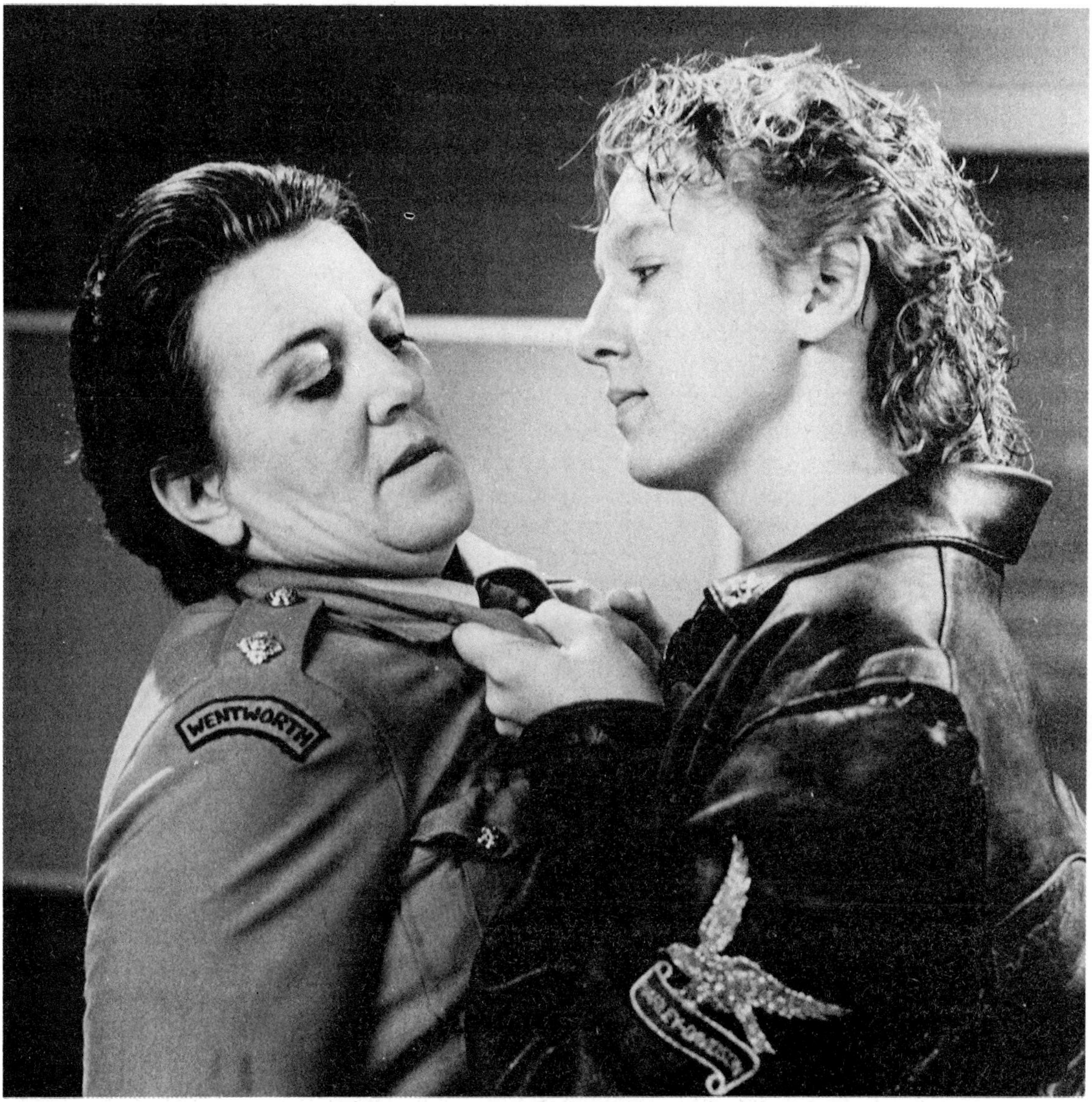

Rita Connors (Glenda Linscott) knows of some 'heavy evidence' against Officer Joan Ferguson (Maggie Kirkpatrick) and isn't against letting the officer know what the career consequences would be ... and for the time being The Freak must comply

fans loved it. Maggie Kirkpatrick couldn't believe the avalanche of mail. 'I should have joined the show earlier,' she quipped. Among the glowing fanmail letters was one from entertainer Sammy Davis Jr. He was a 'Prisoner' addict. 'I love the show, watch it all the time,' he told Maggie when they finally met when he was doing a concert in Melbourne in late 1983. 'I've watched it for years in L.A. Now I've seen you work here. You're a great actress. I love your character Ferguson. And I want to be in the show with you. Somehow they'll have to get this little black dude into the story – they can work that out.'

Sammy was serious about wanting to work in 'Prisoner', but it soon became obvious his American and international commitments and bookings stretched forward for fourteen months and he wasn't due in Australia again for at least three years. Taping 'Prisoner' was out of the question.

Maggie Kirkpatrick said she hadn't visited a prison before starting the show, 'and I'm not about to. I didn't want to colour the role, so I just put on my uniform and have my hair pulled back. I am an actress and not a prison officer. I think that is a line you can draw. I spoke to Sandra Willson, who had done eighteen years, and she said I was spot

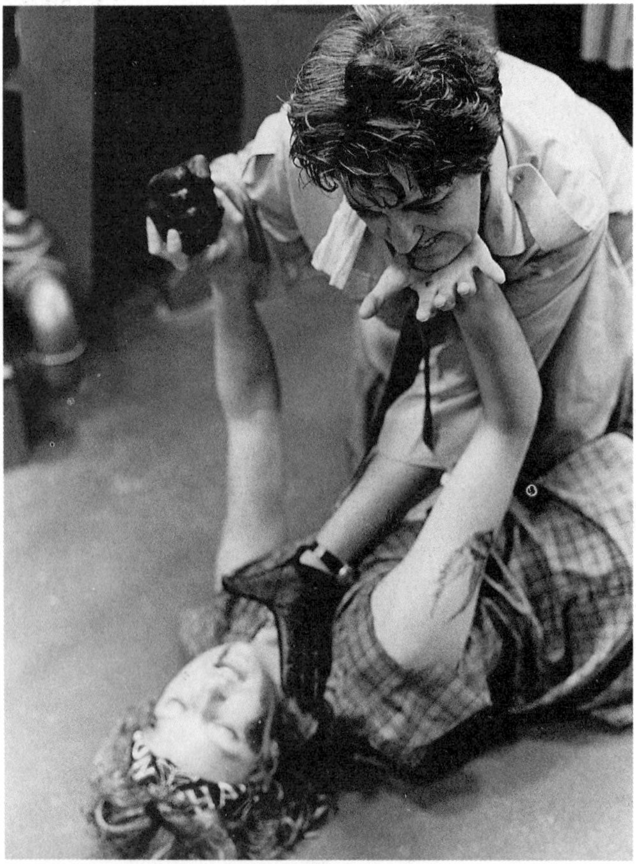

Black-gloved Joan Ferguson (Maggie Kirkpatrick) gets the better of towering renegade inmate Rita Connors (Glenda Linscott) as she metes out her own brand of discipline

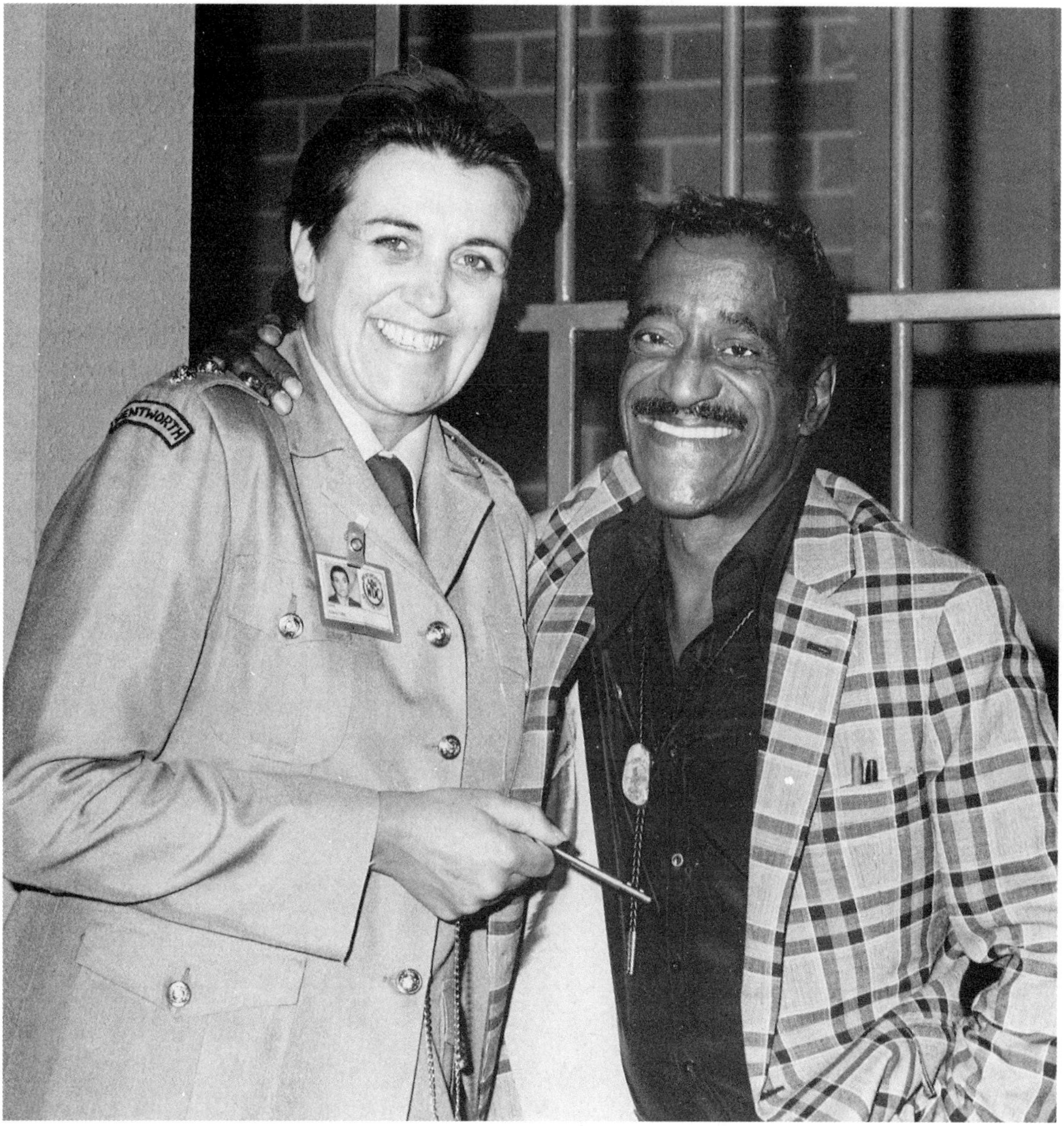

Sammy Davis Jr. wanted to be in 'Prisoner', and asked the producers to give him scenes with his favourite actress Maggie Kirkpatrick. Conflicting dates stopped the deal going through

on, but told me Joan Ferguson must have other sides. I think I got that through to the scriptwriters.'

She certainly did. The Freak had become part of Oz soap folklore. But it was a carefully etched role. She did deal with the baddies, undermined the Governor, arranged escapes, had compassion for a neglected street waif and loyalty to her troubled dad. And Maggie liked the character the better for it.

What she didn't like were the growing number of false reports about her on-screen lesbian relationship with warder Terri Malone (Margot Knight), which was being developed over the middle months of the year. Maggie was furious over media reports which had said there would be explicit lesbian scenes. 'Some reports which came out even before we wrote or filmed the scenes have been garbage,' said Maggie. 'I was adamant from the outset that the affair was treated with dignity and gentleness. There is nothing sensational about it. It goes on out there in the world.

'There must come a time in any lonely person's life when they want people in their lives, whether it be a lesbian or heterosexual relationship. I have insisted the story be treated simply as a lonely person finding someone to communicate with.'

Daily Telegraph (Sydney) entertainment writer Candace Sutton asked Maggie Kirkpatrick why the series 'in its quest for realism and honesty' had not populated Wentworth jail with an accurate representation of Aborigines and drug dealers: 'Good question,' answered Maggie. 'We know most guests of Her Majesty are there for drug-related offences. You're right – where are the drug-runners and black people? I asked for the brilliant Aboriginal actress Justine Sanders [considered by keen judges as the best black actress in Australia over the last two decades] and although it's been bandied around, the powers that be still resist it.'

In fact, Maggie's requests did bear fruit and Justine arrives at Wentworth as learned Pamela Madigan for a special private and personal reunion with returning Governor Anne Reynolds (Gerda Nicholson). It's appropriate timing as Anne has just been jilted by clergyman Dan Moulton (Sean Scully) and needs a friendly shoulder to lean on. Pamela and Anne were great friends at college and radical students of the Sixties.

Maggie Kirkpatrick's main concern, however, was the idolisation of the Freak by youngsters. There were outbreaks of violence amongst Australian kids who proclaimed the warder their heroine. She told Noel Risby (*TV Soap*): 'I'm terribly worried about the repercussions which could arise if youngsters go on taking the Freak so seriously. I'd really hate to think this cult following could spread and get out of control. It scares the hell out of me and I'd like those connected with it to know how concerned I am about their actions.'

Sydney psychiatrist John Fogarty said the reason teenagers look to Joan Ferguson as a cult figure is because they need to identify with persons of superiority. 'People from a lower socio-economic group who have not experienced power in their own right are more likely to associate themselves with a figure who displays it openly.'

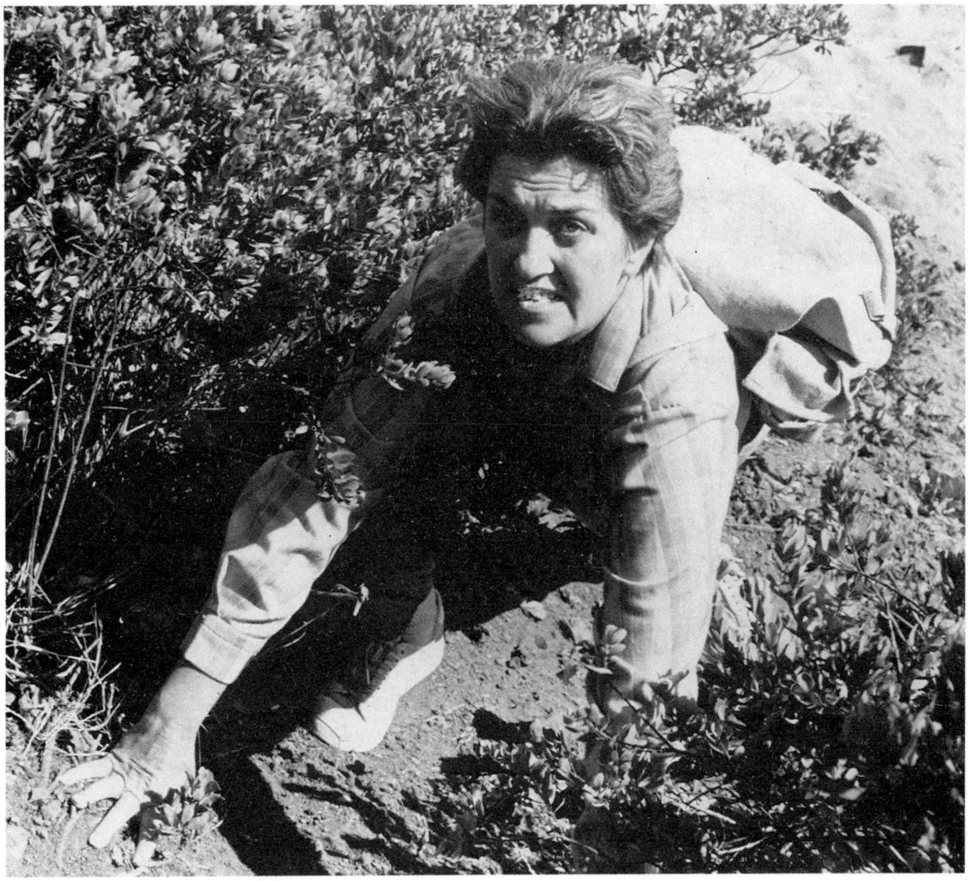

An exhausted Joan Ferguson (Maggie Kirkpatrick) scales a cliff-face seeking help when a work release boat founders at sea. Her prisoners think she's left them to their own fate

Grant Thorburn, of the Australian Psychological Society agreed – but also believed the Joan Ferguson cult amounted to nothing more than adolescent disillusion. 'I think it's because kids have a lack of models to mould themselves on these days. They need a means of escape, but sometimes it's difficult for teenagers to find an adult to respect. It's not a very unusual phenomenon after all. Very young children like to copy Superman or Batman.'

Maggie, though, wanted to nip her cult following in the bud. 'Children wanting to bring the Freak and her values to school as a way of life – that's very much against my wishes. It's something I cannot stress enough.'

PUNISHMENT: PRISONER WITHOUT PETTICOATS

'Prisoner' went off the air in Australia ahead of the usual Christmas-New Year break in 1981 to allow another Grundy series 'Punishment', a male version of 'Prisoner' to go on. It was a programming decision which would seriously harm 'Prisoner's ratings early in 1982 and cause Grundy's untold worries.

Bruce Best, an ABC-TV director with BBC training, was brought in to produce 'Punishment'. Later he would become a top-notch producer-direct or with 'A Country Practice' and 'E-Street'. Despite the input of the mercurial Reg Watson and the best talent Grundy's could muster for the blatant copycat excursion, 'Punishment' laboured through 39 one-hour episodes of banality and lacklustre story-telling.

They couldn't blame the actors. They were some of the best in the country, and even Mel Gibson, about to soar to meteoric heights as one of the world's biggest box-office stars, was lured into Longridge Jail. But it was tame stuff, unable to hit the raw nerve the girls at Wentworth had perfected. Most of the characterisation, including the wives and girlfriends at home, was heavy handed and unsympathetic.

Barry Crocker, who would later sing the 'Neighbours' theme song, starred in 'Punishment' as Superintendent Alan Smith, and Brian Wenzel, now the resilient Sergeant Frank Gilroy in 'A Country Practice', was Longridge's Officer Wally Webber. Veteran Ken Wayne played rough-and-ready Chief Officer Jack Hudson, who liked to put the boot in whenever possible; Ralph Cotterill was a more likeable warder, Russell Charles Davis; American Arthur Sherman was senior inmate Andy 'Pop' Epstein; and Brian Harrison played Sam Wells, in for twelve years for narcotic trafficking.

Cornelia Frances (a top-flight performer from long-running roles as Sister Scott in 'The Young Doctors', Barbara Hamilton, 'Sons and Daughters'; and later in 'Home and Away', as barrister Morag Bellingham) was 'Punishment's' main female interest as the sister of inmate Sam Wells. (Anne Haddy, Doreen Anderson's leukaemia-stricken mum in 'Prisoner', and later to become the Ramsay Street matriarch Helen Robinson in 'Neighbours', played Wells' wife, Alice.) 'Prisoner' buffs will recall Cornelia Frances played solicitor Carmel Saunders during the period troubled housewife Pat O'Connell (Monica Maughan) was tried and held on shoplifting charges.

Some pundits said 'Punishment' got off on the wrong foot when Grundy's proudly announced the author of two episodes of the new show was a former prisoner who is now one of Australia's top scriptwriters. It was left to journalist Don Groves to sum it up succinctly: ' "Punishment" was a lame-duck exercise to try to make "Prisoner" without petticoats.'

All was well on the set of 'Prisoner' as 1982 shooting began at Ten's Melbourne studios. Meg Morris was back in the thick of things, having survived that brush with death in the 1981 cliff-hanger — much to the delight of viewers who had waited nearly three months for the return of their favourite show. But the ratings were down and it was apparent that not only had 'Punishment' sunk like a lead balloon, it had also scared away hordes of 'Prisoner' fans who had found other programmes to escape its obvious blandness.

Pre-'Neighbours' theme-song days for entertainer Barry Crocker as Longridge Prison Superintendent Alan Smith, trying to talk rioting prisoners back to their cells. Armed Prison Officer Jack Hudson (Ken Wayne) stands by. 'Punishment' lasted a mere 39 taped hours

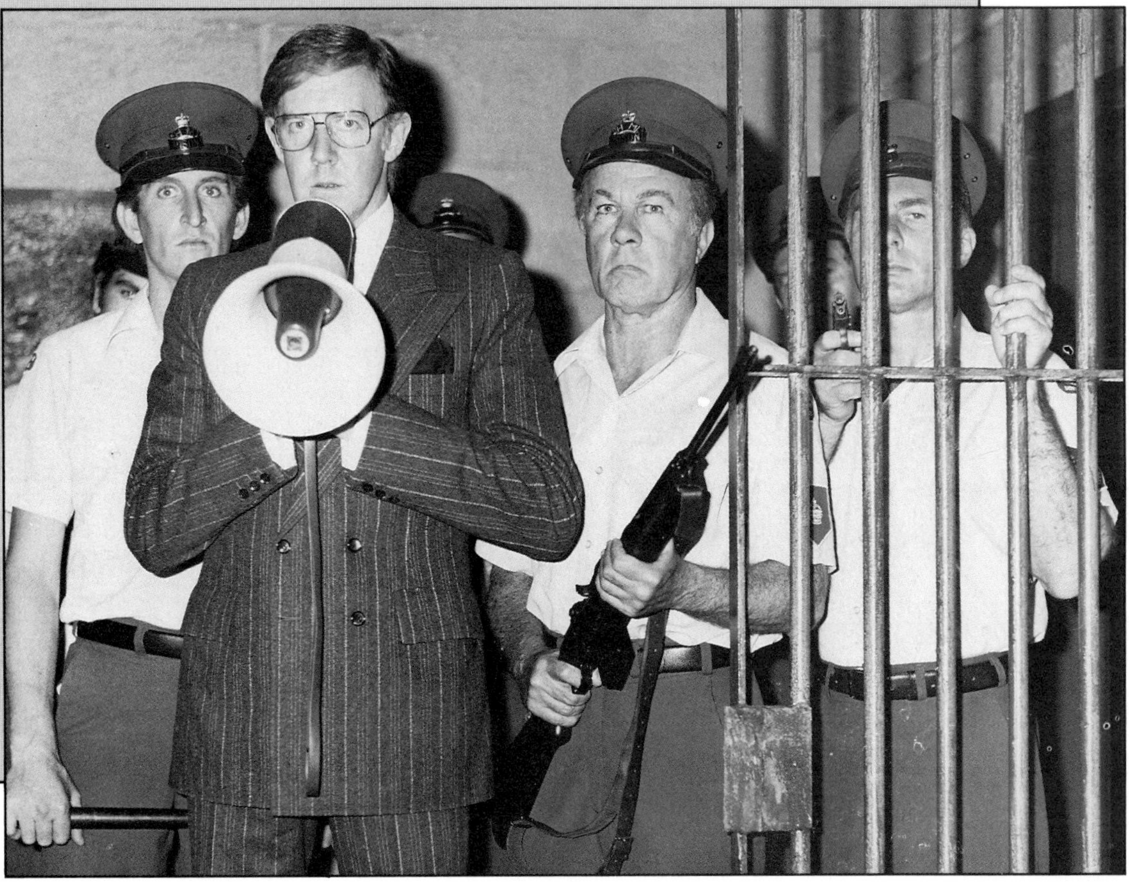

12

CRISIS

The year following the 'Punishment' fiasco, award wins were just the tonic for the girls in Wentworth. It was *TV Week* Logie time once more and Sheila Florance was back among the nominations. So was her best mate Val Lehman – both had been voted by *TV Week* readers as Most Popular Actress on Australian TV, and by a panel of judges as Best Actress in a Series.

Val won both. Her Bea Smith character was still the number one attraction for devoted 'Prisoner' fans around Australia, and had a cult following, although the writers were giving other characters a lot more to do.

Grundy's and Channel Ten (Sydney) were acutely worried about the fall in ratings in Sydney, Australia's premier city [population of nearly 3.3 million, compared to Melbourne's 2.6. At State and provincial level these two big east coast capital cities have had a legendary rivalry as to which city or football code (Aussie Rules or Rugby League) is the greater, which has the better weather, the more beautiful women, better restaurants . . . it goes on and on.]

But what is openly known and agreed in the always cut-throat world of Australian commercial television is that some locally made shows which wow Melbourne are duds in Sydney, or vice versa. Sydney is the jewel of any commercial network, and usually pays the most for network news, drama or special events. So, if you don't rate in Sydney, the harbour city bosses don't like paying the biggest bills. This was precisely the problem facing 'Prisoner' and Grundy's towards the end of March 1982. To add to their woes, two rival soaps from the Seven Network, 'A Country Practice' and 'Sons And Daughters' were doing well and had taken over as the top-rated longest-running drama shows on local stations.

Heavyweight performer Val Lehman, now recognised in all quarters as the official voice of the 'Prisoner' cast, was sent north to Sydney by Channel Ten and Grundy's to juice up publicity and inform the locals that 'Prisoner' was going to be back on top form in coming episodes. And she would have some hard words for Grundy, too.

Val didn't pull any punches at a Sydney press conference. She readily admitted the show was going through a flat patch. 'But that's all about to change. Expect plenty of heavy action real soon.'

Val denied her leave of absence from the line-up (to work on outside drama productions) had played any part in the Sydney dilemma. 'We rate very well in Melbourne and elsewhere, but if you don't perform with figures in Sydney, you're not too safe.'

Explaining that taping was four months ahead of the current on-air shows, Val said: 'The writers and producers are honest enough to know what the problems are, and what has to be done to fix them. Look, I've been in the show for more than three years, from day one. I wouldn't stay unless I thought we were going to deliver the goods and get back to being number one everywhere. We have a top show, unique anywhere in the world, and we're going to make sure Sydney people start tuning in again in the big numbers of the past.'

But the best quotes came when a journalist asked how Val felt about the enormous success of 'Prisoner' in the United States. The firebrand in one of Australia's most volatile actresses ignited. 'The show is seen by 35 per cent of America, you know, and the remuneration for the lead actors is about $70 (£34) a week – and we have to pay tax out of that.'

Val said she was bemused and indignant that after three successful seasons and a string of awards she had yet to meet the principal of the production company which employs her (Reg Grundy). 'I find that so very extraordinary and I think it's a shame we are not in closer contact with the people for whom we work. I think it's one of the advantages of working for Crawford's that they have a man (Hector, the company's founder, and chairman-executive producer) who is so closely concerned with his cast and crew.

'The 'Prisoner' cast sent a letter to Mr Grundy and it was answered by the managing director Ian Holmes. In fact, it took two years before I met any of the Grundy executives. I think it is enormously insulting. And they keep the Logies on their desks.'

In 1982, Dorian Wild (*Daily Telegraph,* Sydney) decided it was time to write an early epitaph for 'Prisoner'. 'There will probably be a bit of head-scratching when this one folds. Although the show rates well in Melbourne, it is rating badly in Sydney. It's not hard to see why. In a word the show is rotten. There is a tiredness about it that would stun even Methuselah. Every prison routine has been worked over and the show has a pervading sense of been there-done that. Enough hair has been pulled to stuff mattresses for every prison bed, enough pills have been pushed to open a fair-sized pharmacy,

PRISONER FILE

Name: Sister Anita Selby

Actress: Diana Craig

Actress Diana Craig had an early role in 'Prisoner' as an escaped inmate before she became Sister Anita Selby three years later. She is arrested at a nuclear disarmament rally and charged with disturbing the peace and inciting a crowd to violence. Her scenes with Sister Mary Helen Sexton (Carmel Millhouse), the superior of her order, bring a new twist to the story.

enough fatuous home-spun philosophy has been spouted to keep Ronald Reagan in speeches for a year. When the steel doors of Wentworth jail swung open in 1979 it was a breath of fresh air. The way things are going at present, the best thing Grundy's could do is open the doors again, let everyone run away and get on with something else. Let's hope they will.'

Another major embarrassment for Grundy's and the O-TEN Network was the contentious gap between Melbourne and Sydney screening dates for 'Prisoner'. National magazines (especially the more regular publications *TV Week* and *TV Soap* – and later *TV Star* – which specialised in 'Prisoner' coverage) gave up-to-date details of what was happening in the show as episodes aired in Melbourne, as well as advising who was leaving or joining the show. Major on-screen events like deaths, riots, romances, babies, paroles and escapes were regular media headline events. Sydney viewers had no chance of escaping the national and local deluge of advance information. So, by the time episodes aired, they were tired stories.

Melbourne-based producer John McRae didn't want to start an inter-city war (and media mogul Rupert Murdoch was now the owner of the network), so he was guarded in his comments. However, McRae did suggest Channel Ten in Sydney 'may be doing something wrong. "Prisoner" works well in Melbourne, Perth, Brisbane and Adelaide.

PRISONER FILE

Name: Marlene Warren

Actress: Genevieve Lemon

Marlene 'Rabbit' Warren, a wild and reckless girl, was seen to have many of the same qualities as Doreen Anderson (Colette Mann). As the result of an idiotic prank, she finds herself in Wentworth for manslaughter -- throwing stones from a train, she hits a driver's windscreen and he swerves, hits a telephone pole and is killed.

Genevieve Lemon played the retarded girl Dawn in Steaming the story of seven women who meet in a Turkish bath.

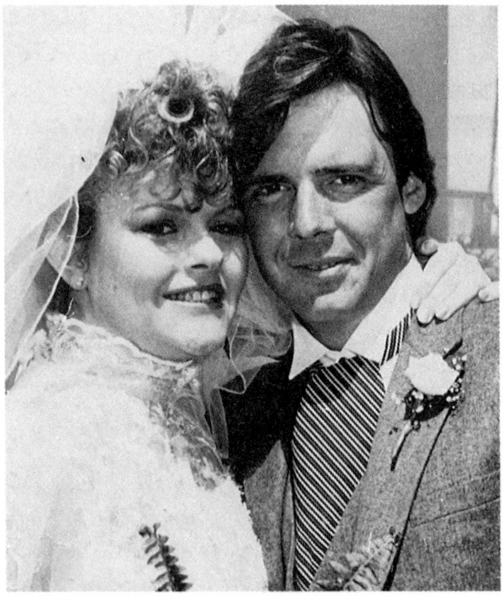

PRISONER FILE

Name: Leigh Templar/Shirlene Chapel
Actress: Virginia Hey

Shirlene Chapel, who called herself Leigh Templar on arrival at Wentworth, got mixed up in pornographic movies. When her mentor refuses to hand over prints and negatives she smashes in his skull with a statuette. Actress Virginia Hey, six foot international model, is best remembered for her role of Warrior Woman in **Mad Max 3.**

In Sydney I hear they take it off for a couple of weeks every now and then for special series or sports events.'

Greg Coote, Channel Ten's boss in Sydney, agreed. 'We have moved it. I think that contributed to its problems a bit. Of course I'm concerned at the Sydney ratings, but this latest batch of episodes now on air is much tougher than a few weeks ago, and will work better.'

Later in the year the sneaky Nine Network created a bizarre case of 'double, trouble' for Grundy's and Reg Watson, who were still trying to win back 'Prisoner' audiences in Sydney.

Nine scheduled their new drama series 'Taurus Rising' against 'Prisoner' in the coveted Tuesday 8.30 p.m. timeslot. Who was producing 'Taurus Rising'? Grundy's, of course! And who supervised the show? Reg Watson, of course. And he was shattered!

Daily Telegraph (Sydney) reporter Campbell Reid wrote: 'It is difficult for Watson to be totally enthusiastic when a rival network contrives to programme his most cherished products against each other. In the days after the celebration for the 300th episode of "Prisoner" he said it came as a tremendous shock to him that "Taurus Rising" was to be scheduled against "Prisoner". For years there had been an unwritten gentlemen's agreement among the three commercial networks not to schedule local series against other local series, and this had been observed with only a handful of violations.'

'It is a far from perfect situation for the Grundy Organization, but we have no jurisdiction over when the shows go to air,' Watson told Reid. 'This has been an emotional period for me. I have a very strong attachment to "Prisoner".'

Asked if the two programmes were competing for exactly the same audience, Watson took a long time to answer. And, when he did, it was a straight 'Yes'. Asked if one was likely to kill the other, the answer was a much less definite 'No'. He didn't believe that. 'I think they can live in the same timeslot. Perhaps, opposites will attract.'

'Prisoner' didn't kill off 'Taurus Rising.' 'Taurus' killed itself. In a way its demise was like 'Punishment' revisited. The tale of two rival wealthy families, the Drysdales and the Bents, it was initially compared to two American shows, 'Dallas' and 'Flamingo Road'. Written by Michael Pate, the two-hour telemovie which launched the 'Taurus Rising' series seemed strong enough, but the subsequent episodes nose-dived to abysmal reception and low ratings. Maybe the Grundy factory had spent the whole budget on the opening show, reported to have cost $580,000 (£276,000).

It was a costly attempt to clobber 'Prisoner', and it failed miserably. So with the 'Taurus Rising' challenge taking care of itself, the mob at Wentworth pushed on with added vigour as Judy Bryant's departure to set up the halfway house neared. Betty Bobbitt confided she had taken several pages of notes when talking with Sandra Willson and discussed them in full with the scriptwriters. 'Sandy told me that Judy must be tough, and always in charge, yet make sure there was always a shoulder for someone to cry on.'

An up-and-down year was about to play itself out, but Grundy's, Reg Watson, producer McRae and O-TEN had learned major lessons over the second half of 1982 and already put into motion some exciting changes for 1983.

It got to the stage that you never knew who would pop up on the screen as 'Prisoner' headed towards its record-breaking 500th episode. Ultra-marathon runner, 53-year-old Cliff Young, appeared on the show as himself, tutoring the inmates on fitness as they organised an attempt to break the world record of 72 hours waltzing to raise funds for little deaf girl Debbie Peters. Potato-farmer Cliff hit the headlines when he won the inaugural Sydney-Melbourne marathon (600 miles) in 1982 with his famous 'gum-boot shuffle' gait.

13

THE KEEPERS II

The 'Prisoner' cliff-hanger, which showed in Australia in 1982, had a fire burning furiously at the Wentworth Detention Centre, and six people trapped inside – an episode which saw the ratings climb significantly. It augured well for 1983, even if it meant almost burning down the place.

The fire was a result of a Bea Smith plan of revenge gone wrong – she herself is in a life and death struggle with the Freak as the fire rages about them. Margot Gaffney (Jane Clifton) created the fire when she threw a Molotov cocktail into a storeroom full of turpentine. Chrissie Latham (Amanda Muggleton) had started a small diversionary fire in the jail library, and at first blames herself for the main fire which trapped the six: Governor Erica Davidson, Bea, the Freak, and prisoners Barbara Fields (Susan Guerin), Paddy Lawson (Anna Hruby) and Mouse (Jentah Sobott). Viewers saw two covered bodies being carried out of Wentworth, the jail a charred mess in the background.

A neat sub-plot for the jail inferno was Fields' attempt to save Ferguson's diary, which Fields has hidden near the centre of the fire. A former shoe-factory secretary, she was jailed for embezzling the firm's money. Now her roving hands hold the key to the volatile confessions and thoughts of the Freak.

The massive fire damage meant the prisoners had to be moved to Barnhurst Prison, the top-security institution where many Wentworth uncontrollables had been sent for varying remedial stretches. The enforced transfer offered a different mood, though life for the jailers and inmates continued much the same.

Wayne Jarratt had left his role of Officer Steve Fawkner to join Mel Gibson and Warren Mitchell on stage at the Nimrod Theatre in Sydney for a special season of *Death of a Salesman*. 'I had an eight-week get-out clause in my contract so I have taken the option and left sooner than expected,' he said when asked about the suddenness of his departure. 'I did three years at NIDA and worked in several plays after graduating. I love the theatre. It has its own magic. I couldn't pass up the chance to work with Mel, Warren and Peter Gwynne.'

Judith McGrath had been badly scalded and burnt on the legs when she accidentally knocked over a kettle of boiling water in the 'Prisoner' green room and had to be rushed to nearby Box Hill Hospital for emergency treatment. 'The poor cameramen had to shoot me from above the hem-line to be sure you couldn't see any bandages. It could have been worse, according to the hospital staff,' Judith said.

The Brisbane actress had come to terms with the 'iceberg' tag that adorned Officer

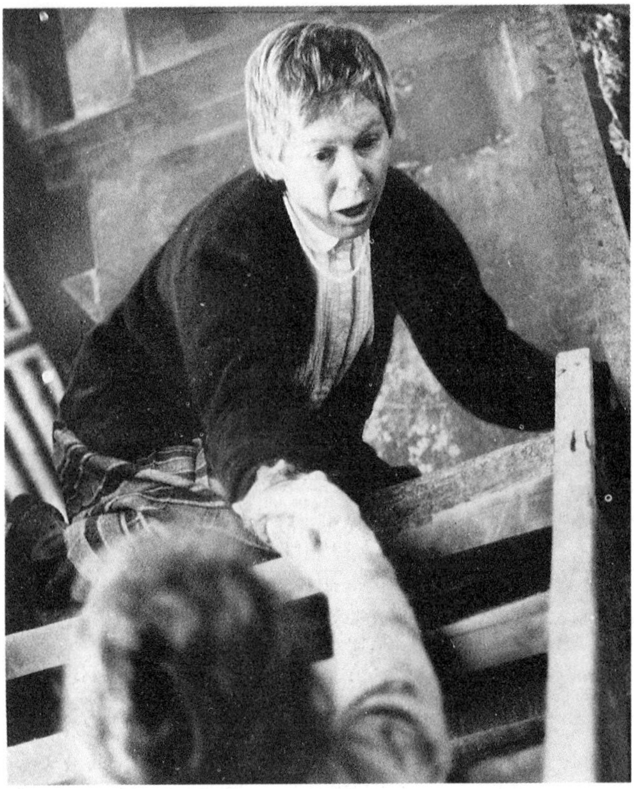

Frantic Meg Morris (Elspeth Ballantyne) grimly hangs on to Governor Anne Reynolds (Gerda Nicholson) trapped in a burning building – the fiery cliffhanger for season 1983

Powell, and made her one of the most identifiable actresses in the land. Judith confessed that the first time someone called out in public, 'You bitch!' she ducked into the sanctuary of the nearest pub.

Early June saw a new Governor at Wentworth: Gerda Nicholson as Anne Reynolds, replacing Erica Davidson (Patsy King). Network O-TEN introduced the new boss in a two-hour special. Patsy King had grown tired of the role and wanted to concentrate on new theatre projects. 'I've been here since day one – one of the few survivors. It's been interesting, hard work and fun. But the time to move has come. I'll

What love will do to a woman. Wentworth Jail Governor Anne Reynolds (Gerda Nicholson) takes to the pillion-seat of a motorbike with beau Dan Moulton (Sean Scully)

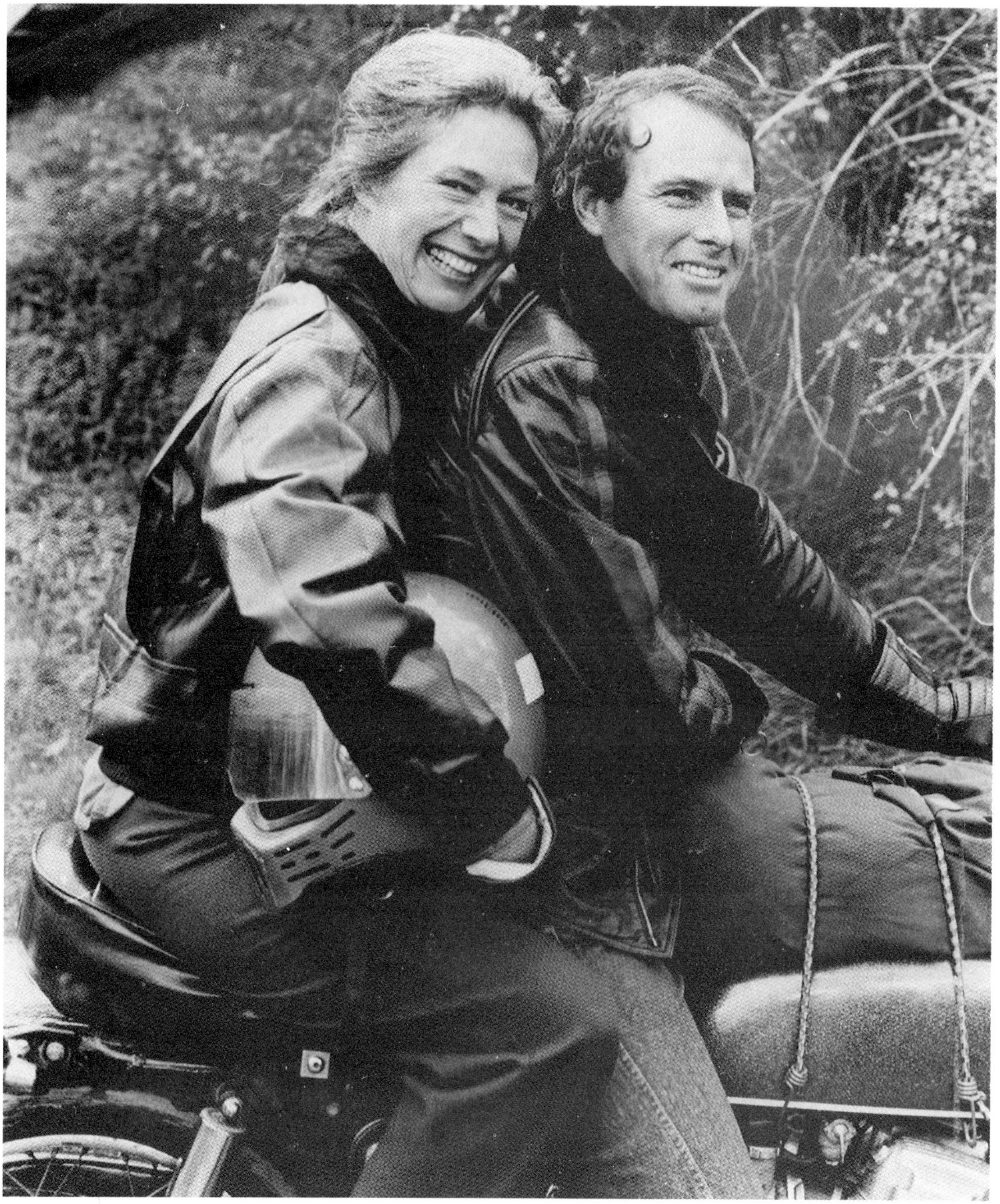

miss the girls and the camaraderie "Prisoner" has provided for so long. I just hope I don't cry too much the day I sign off.'

No such luck on the 'Prisoner' set. The tears flowed.

Gerda Nicholson had impeccable administrative qualifications 'For some reason, Gerda, 46, said, 'I'm always the boss or running things in the film and TV parts I have done recently. In the movie *The Clinic* (which also features Betty Bobbitt), I am the doctor in charge of a VD clinic, and I've just finished the movie *Next of Kin* in which I am a hospital matron.'

Anne Reynolds is given the Wentworth job because the department chiefs think she is going to be a puppet, unlike the previous governor. 'Anne goes along with the authorities because she doesn't see it as being wrong. But she quickly upsets several people because she is so concerned with paperwork. This is my first major ongoing role since a six-year stint as farmer's wife Fiona Carstairs in "Bellbird". I hope this run is as long.'

Joy Westmore was happy that Officer Joyce Barry had earned a heavier workload. 'I wasn't unhappy or complaining about the size of my role. Thankfully, the producers and writers see some value in exploring Joyce at home, as well as in uniform at Wentworth. Viewers are in for a few surprises with her.'

There were plenty of new faces when 'Prisoner's' 1984 unveilings brought the Wentworth adventures back in full flight, with Elspeth Ballantyne's staid warder, Meg Morris, the only survivor from the original cast of five years earlier.

'Prisoner' was back to clean up the cliff-hangers and start another year – so they offered three murders, a vicious assault and a heart attack all in 30 minutes. Governor Anne Reynolds (Gerda Nicholson) had little time to exhale the smoke and clean up her singed locks before she was weepy over breast-cancer fears; and Lizzie Birdsworth (Sheila Florance, still on air, but no longer taping) is again stricken with her ever-

PRISONER FILE

Name: Ethel May Parslow

Actress: Lois Ramsay

Ettie isn't the 'full quid' and has been treated much like a piece of furniture -- since being on remand in 1940, she has been moved around from prison to prison. The records of her case had been requisitioned during the war by the military and her records went missing. When her case comes to light, she is awarded $250,000 (£119,000) compensation from the Prison Department. Later she moves in with Meg and seems for a while to be too happy inviting undesirable derelicts home to wine and dine in style to think about moving on.

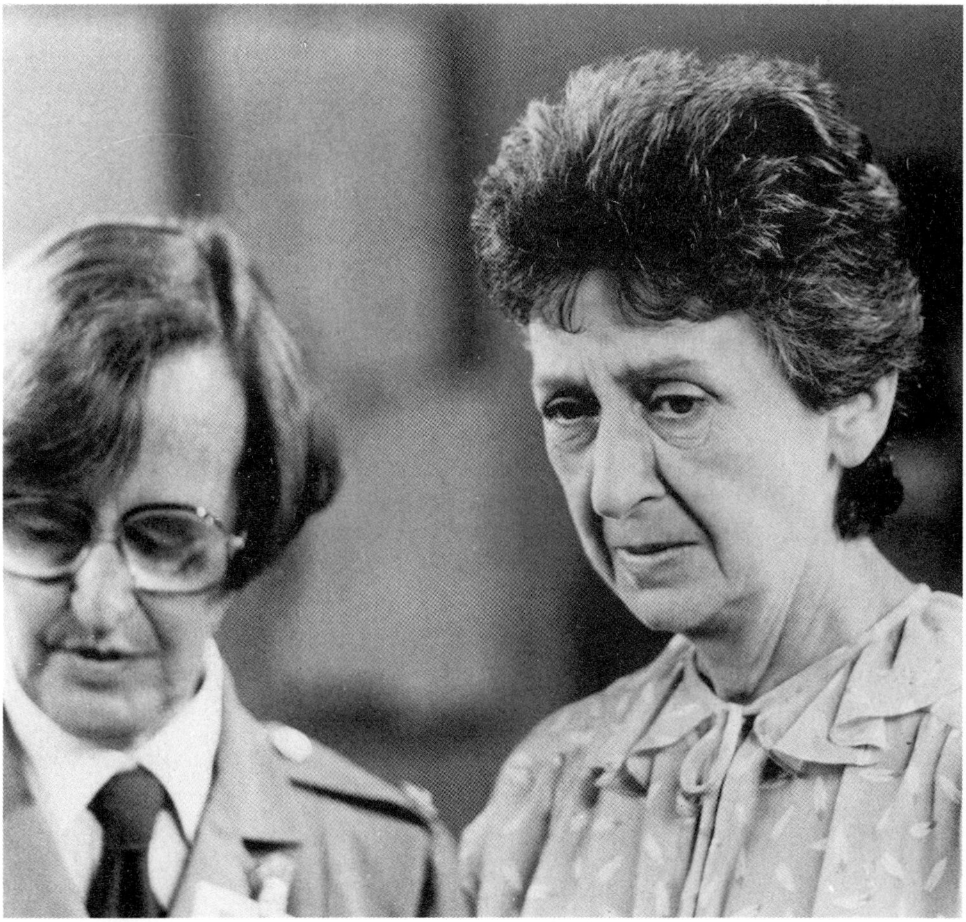

Husband poisoner Edna Pearson (Vivean Gray) is admitted to Wentworth by Officer Joyce Barry (Joy Westmore) — the future gossipy

Mrs Mangel of 'Neighbours' played a character which almost brought unprecedented legal action from a real-life accused poisoner

present chest pains when she discovers some of the bodies littering the premises. Young prisoner Bobbie Mitchell (Maxine Klibingaitis) had tried to commit suicide by hanging.

When the Governor is hospitalised for tests, Joan Ferguson (Maggie Kirkpatrick) takes over as Acting Governor, and cements her power base even more in the boss's absence.

And the arrival of tough new prison officer Rick Manning (played by New Zealand actor Andy Anderson) adds further to the inmates' worries. He has been sent to Wentworth to replace psychotic officer Barry Cummings (Peter Bannister) who killed two inmates before being axed to death by Cass Parker (Babs McMillan). 'By the time his stint is up there are any number of prisoners willing to kill poor old Rick,' said Anderson.

Marie Trevor, 61, one of the most experienced TV producers in Australia, and a former director of 'The Box' and 'Matlock Police' (she was with Crawford's for fourteen years) joined Sue Masters producing 'Prisoner'. (Sue was about to join Jim Davern as co-producer of 'A Country Practice'.) One of Marie's first announcements was that 'three male prisoners from another jail are to be admitted to Wentworth – they're being accommodated there because their lives are in danger, having stopped a mass breakout at their all-male jail.'

At first Governor Reynolds doesn't want the men in her prison, but is told by the authorities that if she doesn't accept their orders she will be demoted and replaced by

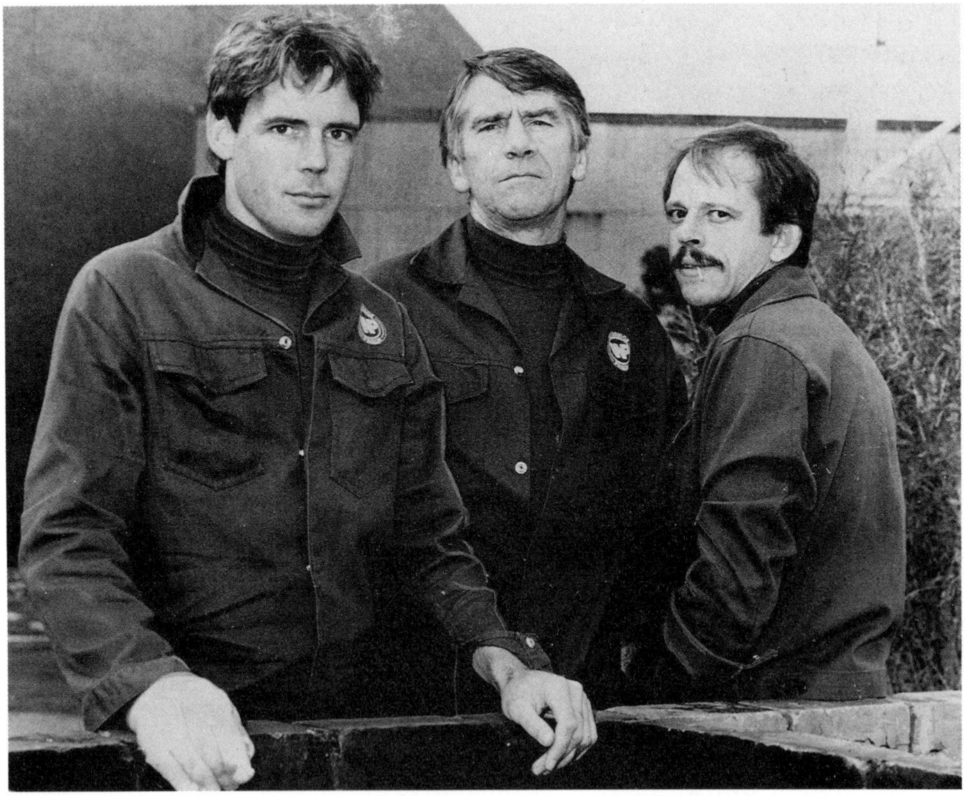

Transferred to 'safer security' for their own protection, Wentworth's first three male inmates (*from left*): Matt Delaney (Peter Bensley), Geoff Macrae (Les Dayman) and Frank Bourke (Trevor Kent). Their moods and passions will change forever the lives of the women prisoners

Joan Ferguson, who made sure she impressed the hierarchy when running Wentworth while Ms Reynolds was in hospital for her cancer tests.

Elspeth Ballantyne, involved in a highly controversial and very physical rape scene, admitted, 'It was one of the most difficult tasks I've ever faced in a fairly long acting career.' In the build-up to the frightening scene one of the prisoners becomes jealous of Meg's relationship with a social worker and organises the attack. The masked rapist does his evil deed and leaves Meg close to a nervous breakdown. She refuses to call the police.

'Meg's had so many things happen to her,' said Elspeth. 'Married twice, pack-raped by female inmates, knifed, shot at and raped by a masked hoodlum . . . and I see by the latest batch of scripts I'm to be locked in a booby-trapped building which is about to explode,' she told *Daily Mirror* scribe David Brown.

Gerda Nicholson admits she knew nothing about women's prisons when she joined the cast of 'Prisoner', and it wasn't until late in 1984 she was shown through Fairlea. 'The inmates didn't say much about the show as they were more interested in my reaction to them. Fairlea is more attractive than the fictional Wentworth, having more light and all its bars painted white. They have musters (roll-calls) quite frequently, so there is less opportunity for them to disappear than in "Prisoner". In a series like ours you have got to have things happening.'

Gerda and her myriad fans would need special sustenance during Episode 500 as she went through her most life-threatening events since becoming Governor of Wentworth. The chilling plot was hotting up – police arrested a part-time maintenance man at the jail after Anne received poison pen letters. But the deadly mail continued, and a parcel arrived – it contained a dead rat. Meg Morris (Elspeth Ballantyne) insists Anne stay at her place, where she'd be safe. Police provide a round-the-clock guard at the house.

Viewers, but not our harassed heroines, were now aware Brian Lowe (Matthew King) was the poison pen culprit, supposedly avenging the bashing of his girlfriend Phyllis Kirk (Reylene Pearce). She was left a 'vegetable' after a maiming in Wentworth

PRISONER FILE

Name: Yemil Bakarta

Actress: Maria Mercedes

Maria Mercedes, the cabaret singer, played Middle Eastern Yemil, car stealer, unlicensed driver and cause of a serious road accident. Brought to Australia for an arranged marriage, it is discovered that she can't bear children and her brutal husband begins a constant round of beatings until she finds the courage to stand up to him.

soon after Anne became Governor. Outsmarting the police guards, Lowe takes Meg and Anne hostage, gagging and binding them in a condemned warehouse which he has booby-trapped with a more than liberal dose of high explosives, all complete with a lethal trip-wire.

An unsuspecting policeman triggers the wire and the building blows up in a tremendous display of smoke, dust and fire. Lowe tumbles to his death on a dilapidated staircase, but inside, trapped by the inferno, Meg tries valiantly to save Anne from the flames.

A male version of the Freak arrived the following year with two other recruits fresh out of officer training school. The new ogre is Rodney Adams, mean as they come and prepared to lie and cheat to get whatever he wants. He'll even humour the Freak to gain ground. Handed this plum role was 29-year-old Philip Hyde, Sydney-born, but a recent graduate from the Victorian College of Arts. He had come straight into his first professional role. Hyde said he couldn't stand the character he was playing. 'Adams is a real bastard, and he'll make enemies on and off the screen very quickly. I'm already dreading going to the shops in a couple of months,' he said.

Marty Jackson, son of Meg Morris, was one of the other two trainee graduates. A blond, headstrong, ex-Navy man, he gave Meg a shock when he joined the department. Marty's dad Bill was killed by Chrissie Latham in a jail riot at Wentworth nearly seven years earlier and Meg is worried inmates will try to take advantage of the mother-son relationship.

PRISONER FILE

Name: Lexie Patterson

Actress: Pepe Trevor

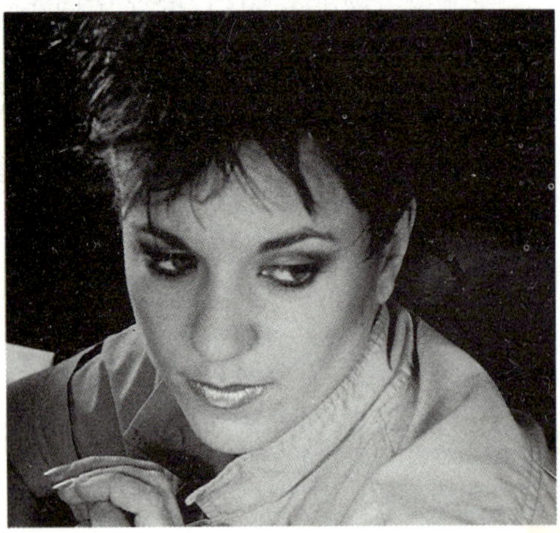

Lexie is the precocious illegitimate daughter of a prostitute and a bit of a card sharp. Looking like a Boy George clone, she is played by Pepe Trevor, daughter of 'Prisoner' producer Marie Trevor -- but she had to audition with 12 others for the role.

PRISONER FILE

Name: Kerryn Davies
Actress: Jill Forster

*One of Australian television's most elegant women, Jill Forster is wife of actor John Stanton (*Taipan, Rent-a-Cop, Naked Country*) and plays white collar fraud, Kerryn Davies. Husband John stayed at home to look after their eight-year-old daughter Polly while Jill was in 'Prisoner'.*

PRISONER FILE

Name: Eve Wilder
Actress: Lynda Stoner

Stunning socialite Eve arrives in Wentworth repeatedly swearing her innocence for the murder of her lover. When her lawyer finally realises the treachery of his lying client, he shoots himself in the head in front of her. And her brutal attack on Officer Joyce Barry (Joy Westmore) leaves her hovering in hospital between life and death in a cliff-hanging end to one run of the series.

Finally, convicted by a kangaroo court of being a lag (informant) and a liar, the crazed inmates led by Lou Kelly put a noose around her neck and hang her, despite frantic efforts to stop them by Joan Ferguson, jail cook Mervyn Pringle (Ernie Bourne) and Officer Steve Martin (Billy Guyatt). But they are overpowered and locked in a cell.

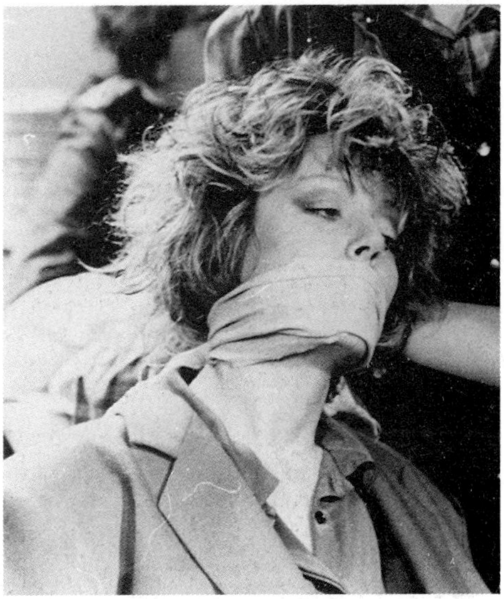

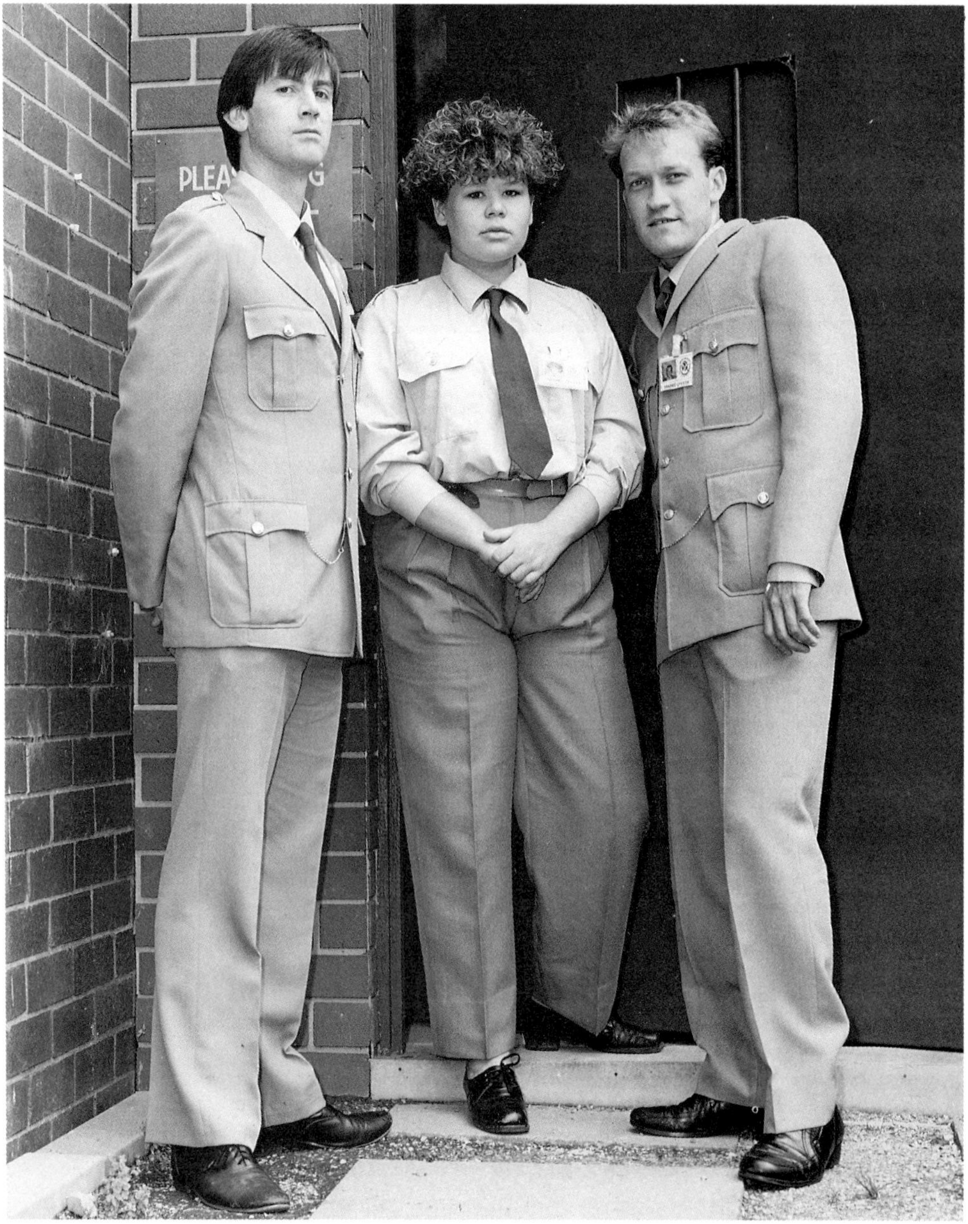

Meg Morris' son Marty Jackson (Michael Winchester), *right*, is among three trainee officers sent to Wentworth for special duties. Rodney Adams (Philip Hyde) and Delia Stout (Desiree Smith) are the other two trainees

The third of the new recruits is hard-working Delia Stout (played by Desiree Smith), who organises work experience programmes which impress the officials and inmates alike. She was in the same intake as Marty Jackson (Michael Winchester) and has fallen in love with him. But he doesn't return the romantic feelings.

The inmates are not prepared for the sudden arrival of Acting Governor Bob Moran when Anne Reynolds goes on leave for 'health reasons'. His iron-fist approach comes from two combat tours of Vietnam, and he immediately declares Wentworth is being run like a local glee club. First to endure his wrath is Rita ('the Beater') Connors, who gets a livid dressing-down when Moran reads the riot act. 'Settle down or you'll wish you were never born,' he tells the giant inmate.

Rita relays the confrontation to fellow inmates describing Moran as 'a dead set mongrel. We're in for a hell of a time while this guy is in charge'.

The softer side of everyone at Wentworth comes to the fore in a poignant storyline that has the inmates organising a fund-raising appeal for six-year-old deaf girl Debbie Peters (played so well by Anna Crawford, daughter of Crawford's Productions managing director Ian Crawford and his charming wife Mercedes). To make her role more authentic, Anna went to the Princess Elizabeth Junior School for the Deaf to learn sign language. 'Now she's teaching it to kids at her own school,' said Mercedes.

14

THE END OF THE THREE MUSKETEERS

The New Year was only a few weeks old when Wentworth's first call-sheets for 1983 were circulated to cast and crew, and the gang again set about producing two hours a week of gritty, jail drama. A month later the stress and strain that before had affected several players got to Val Lehman with near fatal results. Her workload as Bea Smith had been heavy since the series began and, although the producers were giving more attention to other characters, Bea was still a central role.

Val barely escaped death after falling asleep at the wheel going home from a long day's stint at the studios. She narrowly missed a head-on collision with another car. 'We had been filming for nearly thirteen hours. There had been some very heavy scenes and most were very emotional, lots of sobbing, crying, that takes a lot out of you. I came out of the air-conditioned studio into the heat and had to drive home looking straight into the sun. I dozed off at the wheel,' said Val.

'I veered off the road when the oncoming car's horn and screeching of brakes woke me. It was frightening. I just sat there, dazed, feeling helpless. People rushed to my car and asked me if I was OK. I had missed the other car by inches.'

Sitting in the car after the previous night's terror, Val made a vow to herself, her daughters, friends and the show. 'From then on, if I was tired at the studio, and had to drive home, I would take a nap first. I'm not going to kill myself.'

Asked why she was still with 'Prisoner' when her close friend Colette Mann had left, Val quickly ran off a number of reasons. 'I am still exploring some facets of Bea's character. I'm satisfied she hasn't been exhausted. I haven't come to a dead-end. I think Colette felt she wasn't going anywhere new – her Doreen had done it all.' Val added that her new contract with Grundy's meant she was getting more money. 'That's a good reason for staying, too,' she winked.

Val Lehman's brush with death in the car-dozing incident made her relax more on and off the set. At weekends she relished the freedom of 'mucking about' on either of the farms owned by her mother and step-father in south-western Victoria, or on the 'just out of Melbourne' property of her long-time acting friend, Andrew Gilmour. Val did many of the regular farm chores, tending to the cattle, goats, sheep and pigs, either watched or aided by daughters Cassandra and Joanne. 'And I can milk a goat,' says Val

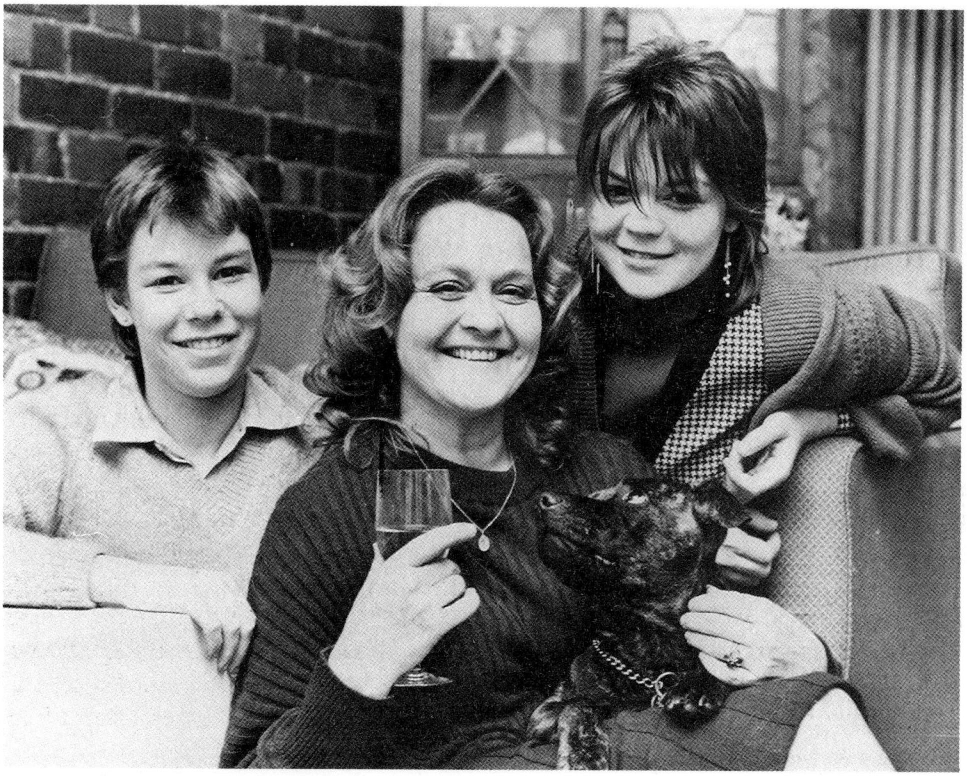

Val Lehman relaxes at home with daughters Cassandra (18) and Joanne (17), and a spoilt canine, Hannah. Cassie had made her debut as a teen drug-addict in early 1979 episodes of 'Prisoner' when she was only 16

PRISONER FILE

Name: 'Weeping Willie' Beecham

Actress: Kirsty Child

Kirsty Child appeared in early episodes of 'Prisoner' as a warder gone bad, jailed and eventually killed off. But she returned as Beecham. 'Willie is transferred from another prison. She inherited her father's disposition for making money by shady deals and is a replica of Lizzie Birdsworth in the tears department -- Willie cries at the drop of a hat. What she lacks in honesty she also lacks in likeability,' said Kirsty.

proudly. 'My ultimate dream is to have a farm of my own. You can't beat being out in the country – all the space, greenery, the fresh air. It's great just to get up in the mornings.'

Other than being down on the farm, Val liked pottering around antique shops, hunting for 'little knick-knacks just as Sheila (Florance) does. I've got this thing about fans,' she says. She owns an impressive collection, one dating back to 1749.

And Val was being seen more and more in the company of businessman John Collins. She was coy about the extent of the relationship, but did admit 'we spend a lot of time together'.

Val was also campaigning actively against drugs. She had made anti-drug commercials for the Australian Foundation on Alcoholism and Drug Dependence. Her two daughters had friends from their primary school days now supporting their heroine habits through prostitution. 'What a waste of two lives,' Val said sadly. Her own life was about to make a dramatic change.

PRISONER FILE

Name: Ruth Ballinger

Actress: Lindy Davies

A villainous piece of work and wife of a crime boss, Ruth Ballinger brings armed terrorists into the jail. Her husband wants Ruth out 'dead or alive' but Ruth knows she won't survive on the outside with her murderous husband out to silence her. So she manipulates the raid to her own ends and in the three-episode siege, the Freak and Warder Joyce Barry are taken hostages, while outside Federal Police, led by Detective Inspector Grace (Terry Gill) argue about sending in the local SWAT outfit.

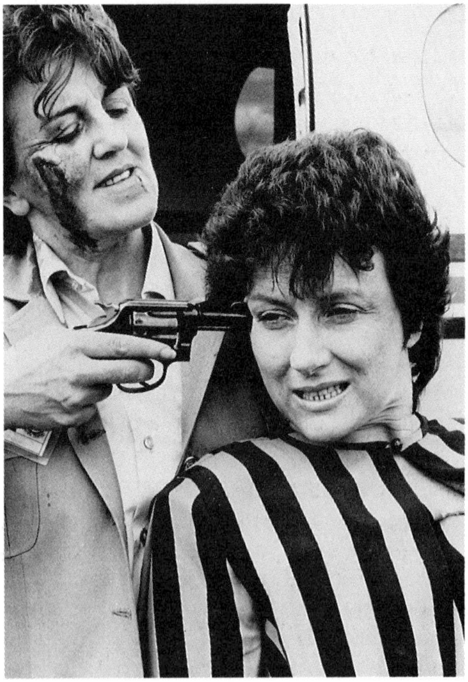

Solo

PRISONER FILE

Name: Lorelei Wilkinson

Actress: Paula Duncan

Before being a Wentworth inmate, Paula Duncan played Detective Danni Francis in the popular Australian 'Cop Shop' series. 'Lorelei was a bright, flirtatious character, a likeable con-woman with a slightly daffy quality,' said Paula. 'Poor Lorelei is nicked for posing as a policewoman -- I guess the scriptwriters are having a go at me.'

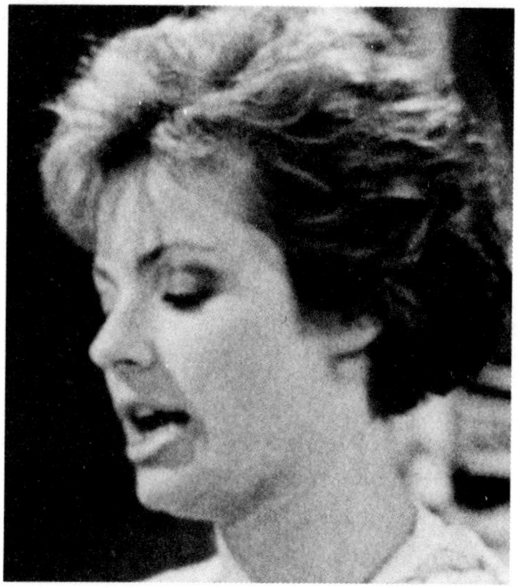

It was drizzling on the morning of Monday 28 March when the shock headlines were emblazoned on newspaper banners outside newsagents and paper shops: BEA TO BE FREED! STAR QUITS TOP SHOW! KEY FOR BEA! 'LET ME GO,' SAYS PRISONER TOUGHIE! STAR: 'I WANT OUT!'

Many industry notables thought the stories were part of a gigantic hoax. One journalist rang a top O-TEN PR executive in Melbourne convinced it was a publicity stunt to try and bring back the high ratings of the previous years. 'I wish it was just that,' the glum PR man replied, 'But she's going. We tried our hardest to talk Val into staying. It hasn't happened overnight. We've kept everything hush-hush for weeks.'

Not since Carole Burns' exit from 'Prisoner' had there been such a public reaction to a star leaving the show. And there was a niggling fear in the minds of O-TEN and Grundy chiefs that a couple of other major stars might follow suit. These fears would soon prove to be justified.

The Melbourne morning radio shows were full of 'Prisoner' viewers telephoning stations to get more information, many wanting the announcers to contact Val personally so she could deny the unthinkable – Wentworth without Bea Smith.

But Val was going. She'd spent several weeks agonising over her decision to quit, and Grundy's and the O-TEN Network had tried to persuade her to stay for at least another year. When that fell on deaf ears, they pleaded for another six months. But Val was adamant. 'Write me out. Kill Bea off. The end has to come,' Val told Grundy's. 'It's time to move on. Four-and-a-half years is long enough.'

Val's agent, Beris Underhill, of Frog Promotions, recalls the furore. 'The phones were hot. No one really believed she had quit. Some callers were crying, and radio listeners were talking about public petitions to get Val to stay. I've been in the business for twelve years and never experienced anything quite like those days.'

Val had two main reasons for leaving. She felt Bea had finally run her race (something she had denied only a few months earlier) and there was a great offer from top producer Wilton Morley (actor Robert Morley's Sydney-based theatrical entrepreneur son) to star in Claire Luckham's new play *Trafford Tanzi*, opening in Sydney in June.

Val dismissed pessimistic forecasts that the series would collapse once she was gone. ' "Prisoner" was never meant to revolve around Bea – it just happened. No one in television is indispensable. They'll find someone to replace me. Life has to go on.'

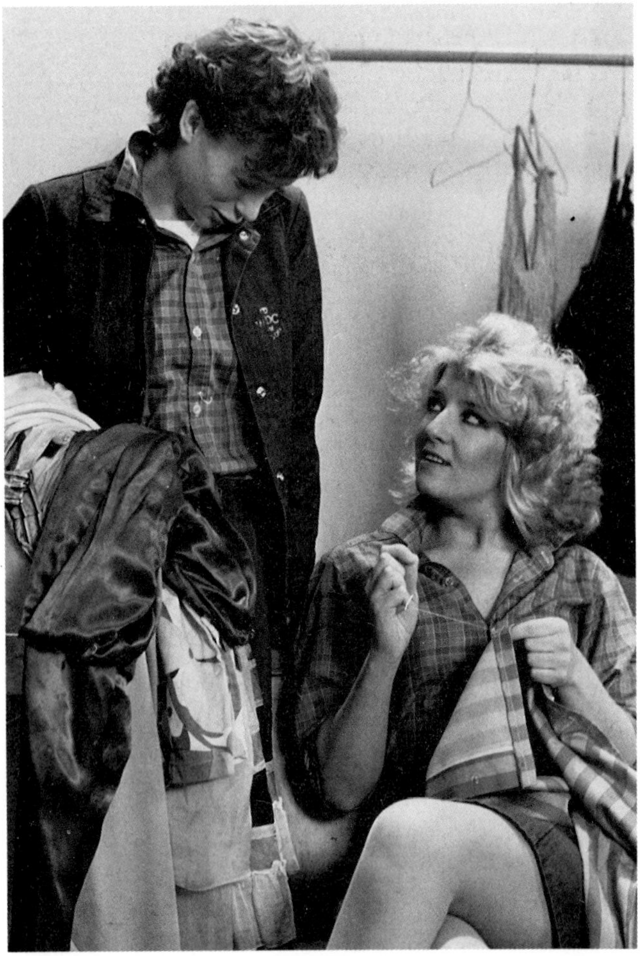

Paddy Lawson (Anna Hruby) and Chrissie Latham (Amanda Muggleton) get ready for the Woodridge Prison concert, a big night for the claustrophobic Paddy, and part of Chrissie's escape plans

Solo

She was firm in her belief that the major factor contributing to the show's continued success was in the strength of the acting performances. 'The cast works as a team, and we help and support each other. The producers and writers welcome our ideas. It's a unique show with unique people.'

Grundy's still hadn't given up on Val Lehman changing her mind about quitting. They seized on a small newspaper story in which Val lamented leaving Melbourne because she would have to give up teaching children drama at a centre in the city. 'Take a few months off for the play, recharge your batteries, go on a cruise, then come back. We'll leave the way open for you to return. Look Colette's coming back, it will be like old times.' Indeed, one of the Three Musketeers was due back. Colette Mann was returning, but for only four episodes to resolve her Doreen Anderson story in the halfway house and settle her parole violations and marriage to Kevin Burns.

But Val stuck to her guns. She'd signed for the *Trafford Tanzi* première season in Sydney, the posters were out and advance bookings were good. The theatre public now wanted a dash of one of television's biggest names.

The only bright light among all this gloom was that the scriptwriters could at long last set up the final showdown between Bea Smith and Joan (the Freak) Ferguson.

It was something of a Black Friday again in Melbourne on Friday 13 May, 1983, when Val Lehman taped her final scenes. 'I don't know who should be more worried about the date – me or the show's producers,' said Val, who seemed to be in high spirits,

PRISONER FILE

Name: Rita Connors
Actress: Glenda Linscott

Rita Connors tough bikie giant (6 ft 2 ins) knew some of the Freak's secrets and let her know from day one that she was going to make things difficult for the head guard and anyone else who got in the way. 'You're scum,' she told Ferguson, her face only inches from the quiet officer's lips. 'Nothing but scum.'

Originally from Adelaide, Glenda was a NIDA graduate of 1978. She joined 'Prisoner' at 27 and had previously found her height a towering problem in getting TV work. She had just played a small part in the mini-series 'Cowra Breakout' as 'the wallflower at a dance who is too tall for all the boys'. The actress had told Daily Mirror *writer, Helen Vines, that when she got the role of Connors she 'went into monumental panic -- not because Rita was a bikie with a boyfriend ominously named Slasher or because she'd slept her way to the dizzy heights of queen of the bikie gang. No, it's because Rita fights like a man and is extremely violent. I'm so repulsed by violence I didn't think I could do it. But all my best friends said it was only a role -- go do it.'*

telling many of the sombre faces to 'get on with it, and we'll have a nice old booze-up at the end of the day – this isn't a funeral.'

But it was difficult for many of the cast on a day when a much-loved mate is about to pack her bags and disappear after more than four amazing years. Val was a very special member of the cast, loved by all, and the crux of so much that had happened in and outside the show. She was its unofficial spokeswoman and she and Sheila Florance were the only survivors from the original inmates. Elspeth Ballantyne was the surviving keeper.

In the end the Freak subdues the seemingly indestructible Bea. Massive audiences across Australia watched the build-up to the battle of the biggies. There are allegations that Bea has planned a major riot and taken control of gambling in Wentworth. Recaptured after her short-lived escape, she is being transferred to Barnhurst Prison and maximum security. For Joan Ferguson and Bea Smith it was a roller-coaster ride to mayhem.

PRISONER FILE

Name: Myra Desmond

Actress: Anne Phelan

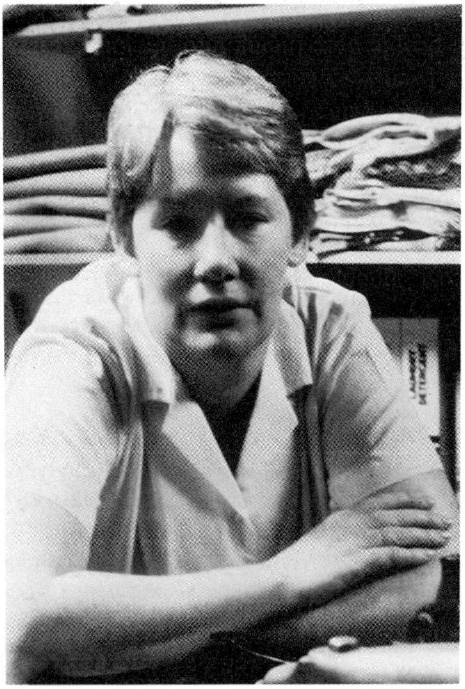

Myra Desmond, head of the Prisoner Action Group, takes no time before she confronts Bea Smith's two worst enemies -- Margot Gaffney (Jane Clifton) and Marie Winter (Maggie Millar). In the end, she takes on the Freak, too, and bashes her into near-oblivion in a vicious brawl, after which the warder needs life-saving brain surgery.

When a crime chief tries to get his wife, Ruth Ballinger, out of Wentworth, Myra gets a stomach and chest full of fatal bullets from his terrorists.

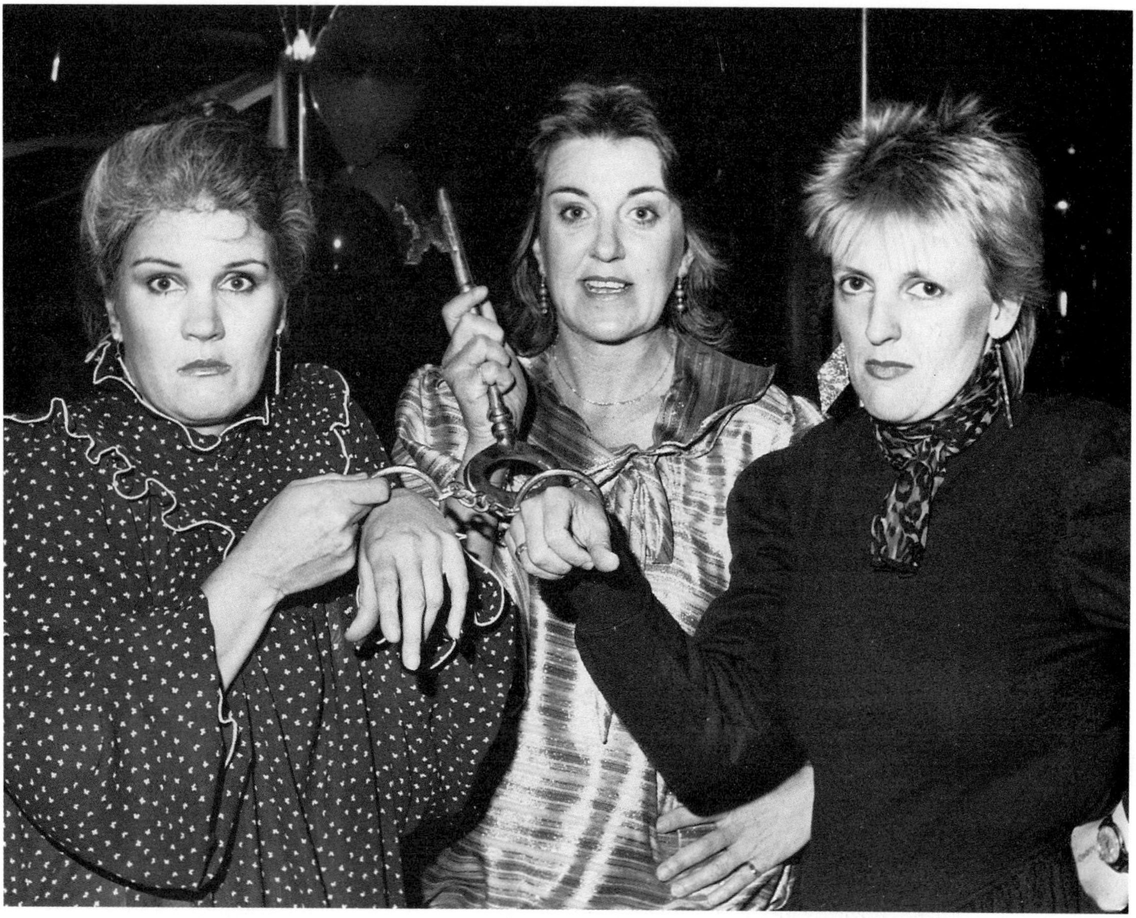

Celebrating the 400th episode of 'Prisoner', and free of their everyday uniforms are Betty Bobbitt, Maggie Kirkpatrick and Jane Clifton. Maggie won the fashion stakes award for the night. In the milestone episode she finally ejects Bea Smith out of Wentworth forever. *(Solo Syndication)*

There was no quarter given, and stunt choreographers assigned to work out the final confrontation between the two bosses at Wentworth stood open-mouthed as Maggie Kirkpatrick and Val Lehman unleashed their brute forces. But Val was leaving the show and Maggie was not – so the Freak was the victor.

That final exchange of looks between the Freak and Bea as the prisoner is carried away on a stretcher to the maximum security of Barnhurst Prison said it all. Then the demented keeper smiled in triumph. 'I had to win sometime,' are the Freak's parting words.

Yet, there were even more memorable moments off camera. The two gladiators collapsed into each other's arms and hugged amid tears for almost a minute before cheering and whistling accorded a magical milestone in Australian TV history. Sheila Florance pressed her way through the throng and took hold of Val's jacket, held on tight and unceremoniously bawled her eyes out.

Several yards away, struggling hard to stop a teardrop or two, was a top Grundy's executive. He had been in the business twenty years, and thought he was pretty tough. Now he struggled against his emotions, and when he saw frail Sheila Florance noisily shedding the most tears, clinging desperately to Val, he knew the writing was on the wall. Colette Mann had gone, now Val Lehman – how long before the last of the Three Musketeers would say adieu? Sadly, the answer was that Sheila was to follow very soon.

PRISONER FILE

Name: Nikki Lennox

Actress: Vicki Mathias

A tough 15-year-old (actually played by 13-year-old Vicki Mathias). Nikki is a tart who rules the streets of her suburban home with a gang of three willing followers (Roby Frank, Nicole Dixon and Liz Bermingham). Her episodes were used as the basis for discussion groups throughout Australia about the English/U.S. scheme, 'Scared Straight'. The idea is that young offenders go to jail and learn about life on the inside. 'Prisoner' scriptwriter, Ian Smith (later to become harrassed Harold Bishop of 'Neighbours') said, 'Studies found it is not the bars or restrictions which terrify the young offenders, it is the tough crims who are in jail for a long time.'

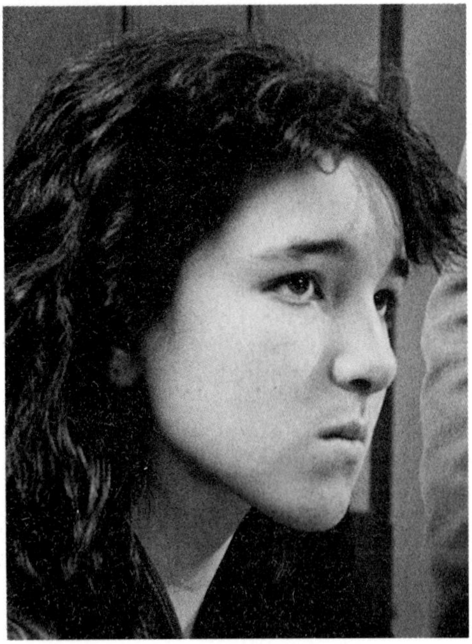

15

THE FINAL TURN OF THE KEY

In mid-February 1986, about 100 special guests celebrated 'Prisoner's' 600th episode at the trendy Petty Sessions restaurant in Melbourne. Tables were decorated with cell-block candle holders and specially printed newspapers highlighted the history of the O-TEN series which by now had employed more than 2,340 people since first going to air on 27 February 1979.

The menu included appropriately, Oysters Kirkpatrick, Lexie's Limp Lettuce, Freak's Friday Favourite and Ferguson's Delicacy with Trembling Tart. Glenda Linscott ('Rita the Beater') won the Most Glamorous Inmate of the Night Award, while Elspeth Ballantyne (the only survivor from day one) was given a special thank you award to a momentous standing ovation.

Grundy's president, Ian Holmes, presented Elspeth with an inscribed silver tray and told the assembly if all 600 hours of 'Prisoner' that Elspeth had appeared in were all unspooled and put together end-to-end the tapes would reach from Beirut to Istanbul, or Jakarta to Singapore. 'We are currently being seen in nine countries with peak viewing numbers around 39 million, and the show has won twenty-one awards,' said a proud Holmes.

But rumours were filtering in from Sydney that O-TEN had told Grundy's that 'Prisoner' would be cut before it reached its 700th milestone. There were strong denials from both O-TEN and Grundy's that the end of Wentworth was near. (In effect, there had been a meeting of worried minds between the network and producers. They had decided to adopt a 'let's see what happens with the ratings' attitude before making a definite decision on the show's future.)

Grundy's upped the action in an attempt to build the fading ratings. First, Lou Kelly busts out of Wentworth and goes on a rampant blaze of carnage up-country after she reaches the Watkins' farm (home of Lurch's family), culminating with the double-murder of Lurch's mother and brother.

Then high drama on the high seas gave some fast and furious action for several members of the cast. Trainee Officers Marty Jackson and Delia Stout convince the authorities that selected inmates should be allowed to gain work experience on the boat 'Wattle', sailing around Port Philip Bay. Chosen are Rita Connors (Glenda Linscott),

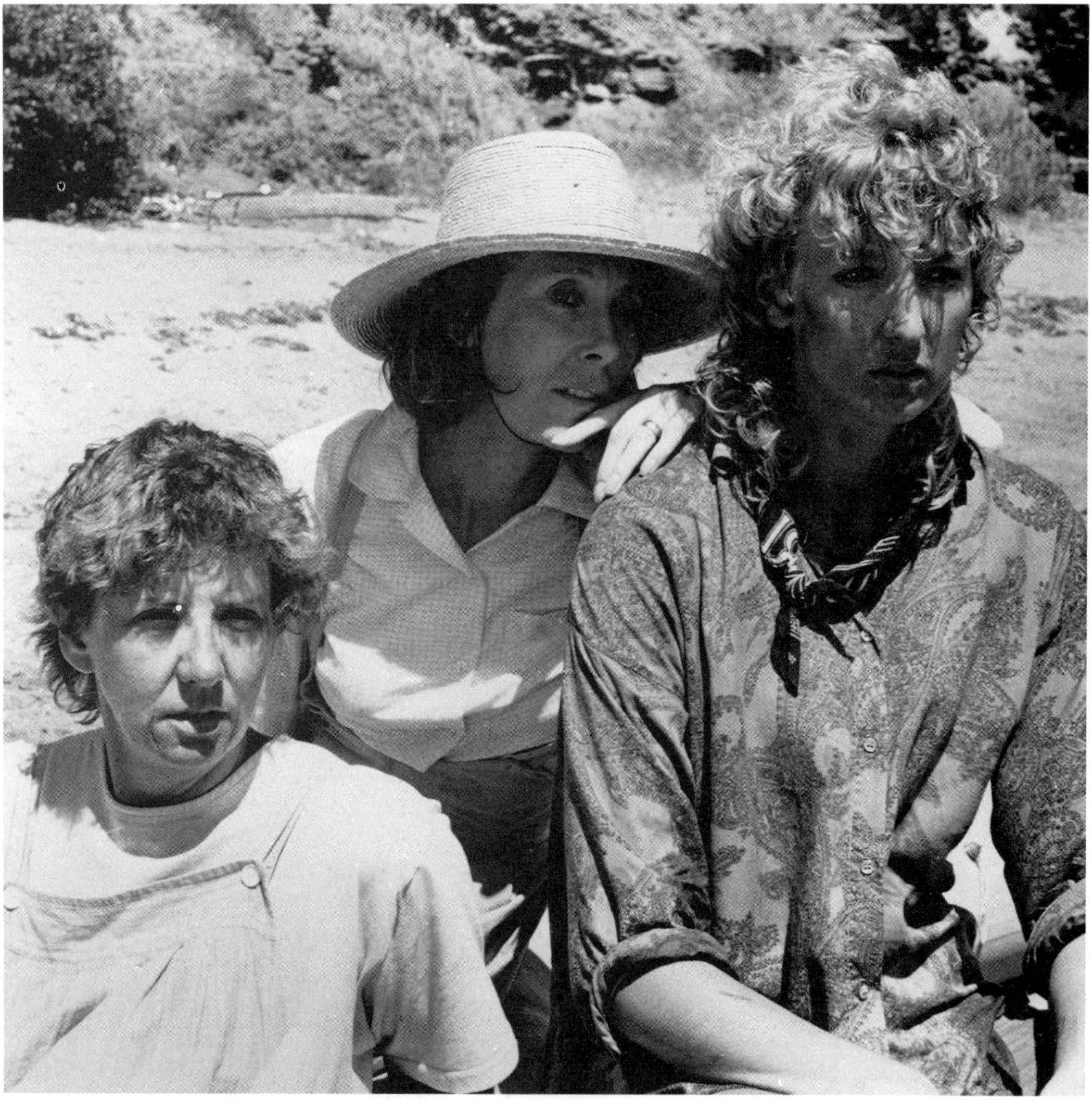

Stranded on a beach after being lost at sea, Alice Watkins (Lois Collinder), Nancy McCormack (Julia Blake) and Rita Connors (Glenda Linscott) wait for a helicopter to lift them to safety. A dismal end to a work release programme on a boat

Alice Watkins (Lois Collinder), Nancy McCormack (Julia Blake) and Lorelei Wilkinson (Paula Duncan). But Lorelei changes places with 'Roach' Waters (Linda Hartley) after day one. The accompanying officers for the trips are Marty Jackson, Delia Stout and Joan Ferguson.

Rita is out to get the Freak, as she believes Joan is responsible for her bikie boyfriend's death. Rita sweet-talks the boat's deck-hand Mick Warner (Nick Caraffa) into tricking Delia and Marty into leaving the craft. She then sabotages the boat's radio. Nancy thwarts Rita's attack on the Freak, who has decided to row ashore for help. Rita swims after her, still intent on revenge and the Freak's death. When they reach the distant shore it is Rita who needs rescuing, and only the timely help of the Freak saves her. Back on the boat, 'Roach' and Mick are falling in love and decide she should escape from Wentworth. Her plan is very clever, but full of danger and makes for one of the show's most extraordinary getaways. And she isn't caught . . .

In spite of all the excitement, 'Prisoner' never made it to Episode 700. The official announcement that the show 'was closing down, having run its course' saddened the cast, crew and mainstream viewers alike. But it was no surprise to many of the principal players, especially Elspeth Ballantyne and Maggie Kirkpatrick.

Maggie: 'I would have been shocked had they re-signed for thirteen or twenty-six more episodes. I felt the show had run its race, and I had already started looking for something to move on to – you've got to finish sometime.'

Elspeth: 'I'm not at all unhappy it's finishing, for the past couple of years when I've seen a friend in the theatre or a mini-series, I was green with envy. I was the luckiest person around when they cast me in the show. It's been a fabulous eight years. Great mates to work with and so many fine actresses. "Prisoner" has given me some of the most memorable moments of my career. But I don't want to be Meg Morris collecting a pension cheque at Wentworth. There's a lot of life left in me and many challenges I want

PRISONER FILE

Name: Barbie Cox

Actress: Jayne Healy

According to actress Jayne Healy, 'Barbie's bit of a screwball. They sort of tolerate me and, luckily, Barbie gets taken under the wing of Rita Connors (Glenda Linscott) and so no one is game to try and harm me.' Barbie is something of a mystery and no one knows why she's inside.

Jayne's one regret about her role in 'Prisoner' is that most of her family cannot hear her in the hit show -- 'Of the six members of my family only the two eldest children can hear. They are terribly pleased for me, but it's a pity they won't know what I say.'

PRISONER FILE

Name: Nancy McCormack

Actress: Julia Blake

Quiet, demure Nancy was found guilty of her husband's murder. But the real story was that she had taken the rap for her son after a fight between the two men had resulted in the death of her husband. Nancy had hidden the body in a backyard grave and told the police it had all been an accident.

PRISONER FILE

Name: Lisa Mullins

Actress: Nikki Paul/Terrie Waddell

Prostitute Lisa Mullins signs in after being found guilty of trying to blackmail an underworld heavy. She arrives obviously frightened the crime boss might send someone after her and she has to watch her back day and night.

After only six episodes, Nikki Paul was struck down with glandular fever and was replaced by Terrie Waddell.

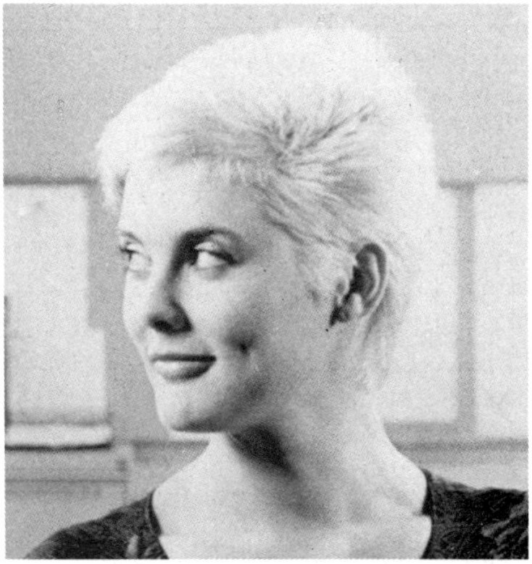

PRISONER FILE

Name: Jessie Martyn

Actress: Pat Evison

Pat Evison, the New Zealand actress, played proud prostitute Jessie Martyn. She discovered that at home in N.Z. 'Prisoner' was the most videoed programme in the country.

to take on. There are my two growing boys – and there's a lot happening away from Wentworth.'

The headlines appeared at once: PRISONER AXED, GOODBYE, WENTWORTH, TOP SHOW CANCELLED, PRISONER SHUTTERED.

In Australian television annals, 'Prisoner' had held its own with nearly 700 hours of drama, over eight years. 'The Sullivans' lasted seven years for its output of 1,114 half-hour episodes (557 hours); 'Number 96' aired for five-and-a-half years and 509 hours; 'Cop Shop' lasted six years for its 623 one-hour episodes; 'The Young Doctors' ran seven years for 622 hours. But the granddaddy of them all is 'A Country Practice' – at the time of writing the Wandin Valley folk were taping their 769th hour in nearly eight years of top-rating Oz soap, and will eclipse the current record-holder, the Reg Watson-created Grundy show 'The Restless Years' (781 one-hour episodes).

Friday 29 August, 1986 was W-U Day on the set of 'Prisoner': Wind-Up Day as the cameras taped the final scenes, and the sets came down, literally tumbling around the

PRISONER FILE

Name: Merle 'Looney' Jones

Actress: Rosanne Hull-Brown

The introduction of Merle into Wentworth caused a furore when critics and the producers differed on how far the mentally retarded character could be taken. Viewers were sympathetic and professional observers felt it was an area previously neglected. Actress Rosanne Hull-Brown said, 'I was horrified when I first read the breakdown of the character. They described Merle as unloved, aggressive and dangerously violent. She only read comic books and had a vocabulary of two-syllable words. Her imprisonment might have seemed harsh, but bit-by-bit her lot improves and she benefits along the way. I think we've handled her just right.'

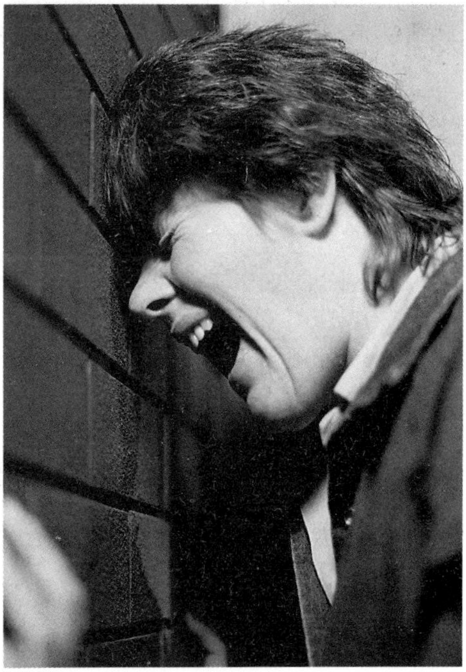

cast and crew. Lois Collinder remembers doing a scene in the laundry, then moving to a corridor for some small pick-up shots. 'When we came back less than two hours later the entire laundry set was gone, down to the smallest prop. Walls were being cut away and carted down the hallway by the art people in their noiseless sneakers. It was like a giant wrecking team and burglary gang were on the job.'

Maggie Kirkpatrick: 'It was sad, almost like being part of a funeral. It was a hectic last day, as there were so many scenes to shoot. We all did what we had to do, told a few jokes to each other as the hours went by. Naturally, the end-of-shoot party was a big event. We had a deserted studio to ourselves, I had a hangover for two days.'

Nearly 3,000 viewers wrote to Grundy's and the O-TEN Network to offer their condolences at the demise of 'Prisoner', and all said they would watch the show to its end – the last 30-odd episodes would screen in Australia during the early months of 1987. Many wanted to start a petition to have production continued, and some offered to launch an appeal for money to keep the prison alive.

Ian Smith, associate producer at the show's end – he had been with the series since episode forty when he was a script editor – said; ' "Prisoner" was one of those rare shows where actors would ring and congratulate the writers on the script, and writers would often call the actors and thank them for the way they worked on certain episodes.'

PRISONER FILE

Name: Lou Kelly
Actress: Louise Siversen

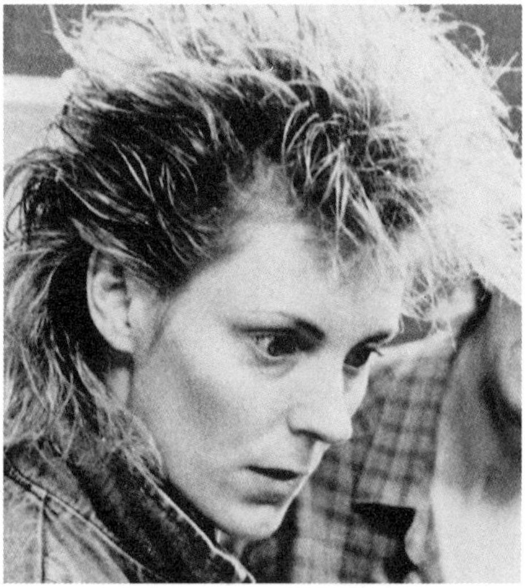

Solo

Lou was a no-holds-barred prisoner who saw life in jail as almost a holiday camp. She got the other prisoners working her way and her worries were over. Her death in solitary confinement was the biggest mystery in years at Wentworth. She had survived several attempts to dethrone her as top dog and there was no shortage of suspects.

Smith, who co-wrote the final episode with producer Marie Trevor, continued, 'Over the many years we had every emotion in the world to play with. Prisoners dream of strange things. They dream of sleeping in a room with the door open. We had all these sorts of things to work off. "Give me my own space," was the catch-cry of the prisoner. The lack of space often causes riots. Tensions build and build. The bells ring, the doors don't just close, they clang shut!

'We had a prisoner on set in the early days to talk about prison routine. He stood in front of a closed door and would not open it. He was waiting for one of us to open it for him, because in prison you don't open a door.'

But the last door had closed at Wentworth.

16

EPILOGUE: BY THE REAL PRISONER

Over the years much has been written about 'Prisoner', and many people in high places in Australia's government and penal reform have had their say, often damning the series. The Oz critics generally got it right ahead of millions of avid viewers in Australia who readily attested to its popularity over a staggering seven years.

It is fitting that the 'real prisoner', Sandra Willson, should have the final say. She's been there, and done it all. This is what Sandra wrote in the *Sydney Morning Herald* of 28 September 1987:

'The final episode of "Prisoner" is being screened tonight on Channel O-TEN and the last two hours will be shown as one episode. It is a time of mourning for fans devoted to this show.

'A number of long-term prisoners who had been released from prison, including myself, were interviewed for authentic material, so this is a nostalgic time for me. I can divulge a few secrets: Wentworth Detention Centre, although filmed in Melbourne, was based primarily on Sydney's prison for women, Mulawa, where the cellular living conditions were similar.

'Although the general warning "no resemblance to the living or the dead" is always screened, there were real characters and factual events beneath the cosmetic, artistic and condensed versions being aired. Peta Toppano and later Betty Bobbitt played roles which were based loosely (very loosely) upon myself, while the halfway house run by Judy Bryant (Betty Bobbitt) was based, again loosely, on the halfway house for ex-

'The Real Prisoner,' Sandra Willson, the longest-serving woman inmate in Australia's penal history. Served 18 years for the murder of a taxi-driver, and was a series consultant to 'Prisoner'. Some of the main aspects in the characters of inmates Judy Bryant and Karen Travers were based on Willson and her exploits. *(Barry McKinnon)*

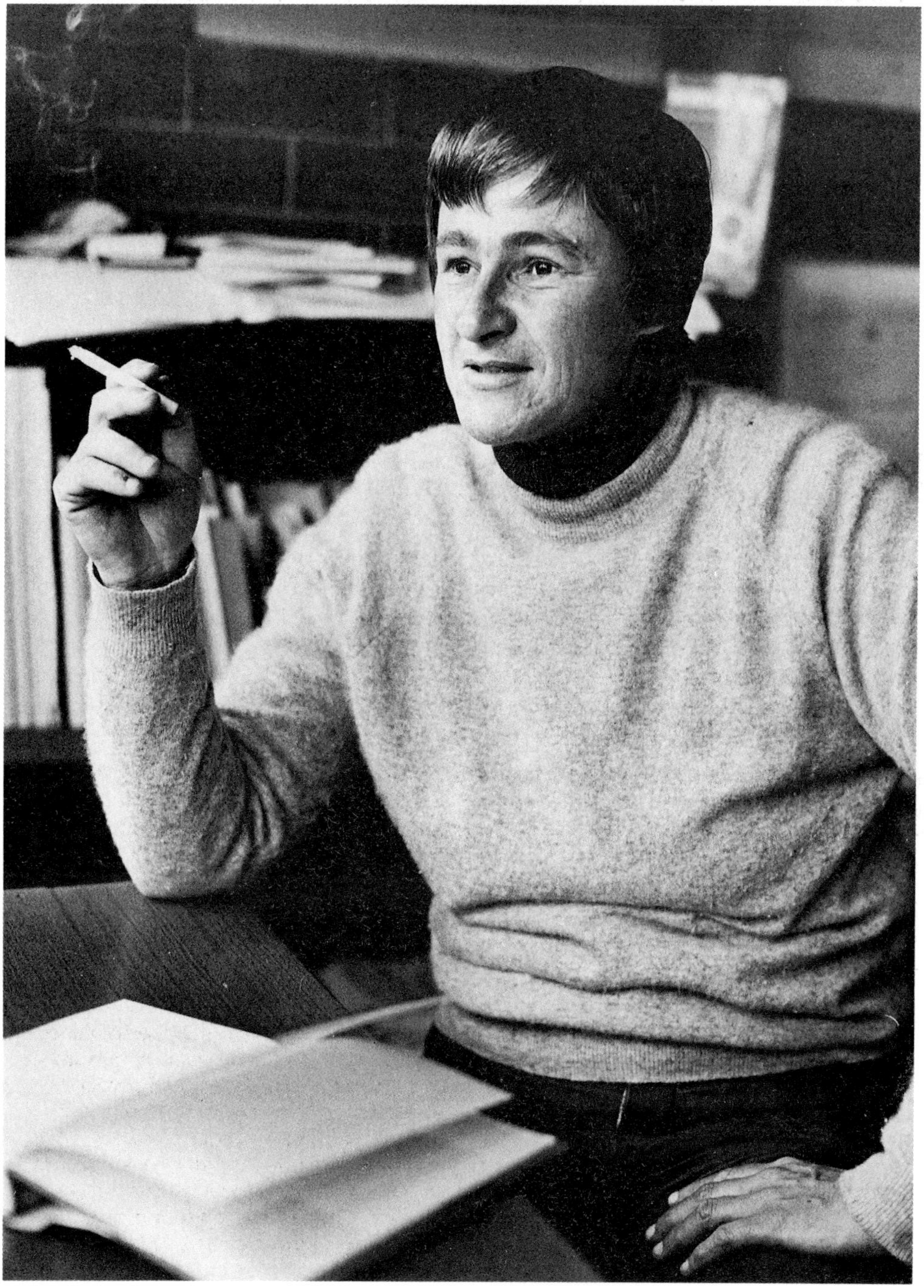

prisoners which I run in Sydney. Certainly my memories of meeting with Betty, Elspeth (Ballantyne) and Val (Lehman), as well as so many others constitute one of the highlights of my freedom.

'If viewers ever thought "Prisoner" was raunchy, just let them think what reality would have been like. The show's popularity stemmed not from the prison angle – although that was an ideal setting to confine the characters for so long – but from the humour it would inject into situations which otherwise would never be viewed as funny.

'The fires, the assaults and escapes were applauded because they reflected the underdog's attempts to get square, to fight back. It was ultimately a series about the underdog, ever an Australian hero. Or, in this case, heroine.

" 'Prisoner" had a long and vigorous run, and opened a fresh avenue for presenting a taboo subject – real prisons and real prisoners do not gain much public sympathy.

' "Prisoner" also introduced many new faces and new talents to viewers. Chief among these was Vinegar Tits (Fiona Spence), who never received a Logie Award for her portrayal of the repressed, acidic "bad" screw.

'I would have survived in Wentworth Detention Centre, but I wouldn't have liked it. I'm opposed to hard drugs, but illicit stills bring back memories . . .

PRISONER FILE

Name: Nora 'Outback' Flynn

Actress: Sonja Tallis

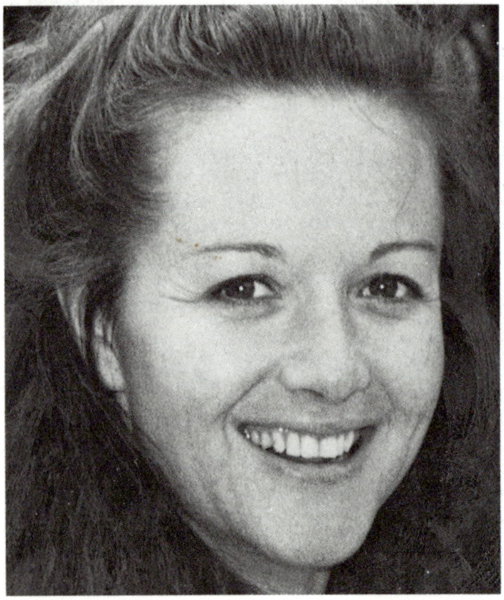

'Outback' Flynn, played by former folk singer Sonja Tallis, has been in jail for 23 years. She appears in Wentworth charged with the murder of three hitch-hikers and rapidly makes it to top dog status -- only to have her career cut short by vicious Reb Keane.

PRISONER FILE

Name: Marilyn Mason

Actress: Margaret Laurence

Nymphomaniac Marilyn Mason was not a role cherished by actress Margaret Laurence. In 1980, while she was in the U.S. looking for new work, she also toured American cities promoting 'Prisoner'. She told reporters that her character in the show 'was terrible. I never thought it would make it here. Margaret Laurence is not at all like that dirty little tart Marilyn you see on the screen.'

Her sultry looks also caused comment. 'I'm tired of people remarking on my similarity to Farrah Fawcett and Brigitte Bardot -- boring, how ghastly. I can act and that's the difference.'

Colleagues back home were not amused, though Margaret complained she'd been misquoted. Val Lehman got straight to the point. 'I am unhappy that an actress can condemn a series just because she is unhappy with her own character.' And Fiona Spence: ' ''Prisoner'' is not one-dimensional. All sides of a character are shown and I believe that is why the programme is such a success -- because it's believable.'

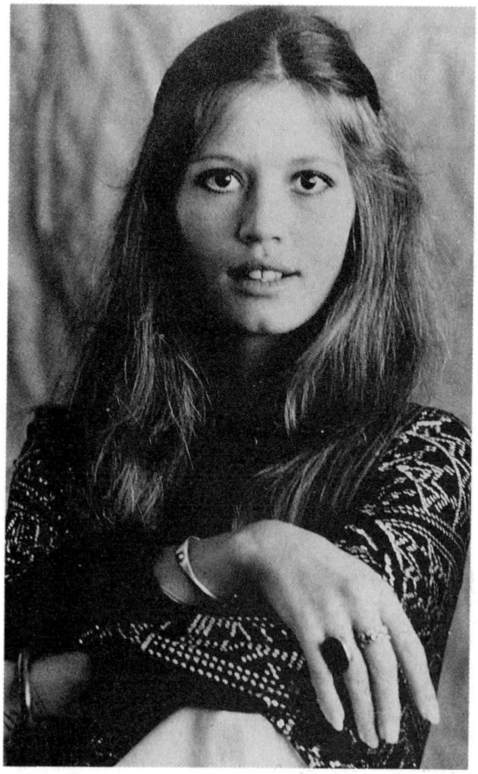

'The bashings? Well, anything in a good cause, as they say. The suicides? Many, horrific. They remain with me today. There is no life within prison walls. It is merely a waiting, a standing still, a marking time. Life resumes only when one is released. Only now am I living, and I will be content to see prison through the eyes of programmes such as "Prisoner". It is better that way.'

Sandra Willson is the co-ordinator of Guthrie House, a half-way house for prisoners, and was in Mulawa Jail between 1959 and 1977. This feature is reprinted by kind permission of Ms Willson and the *Sydney Morning Herald.*

WHERE TO WRITE TO THE STARS

Because the 'Prisoner: Cell Block H' series has finished production in Australia, sending any mail to the studio in Melbourne or its sister station in Sydney is not advised. Likewise the production company, which doesn't have the facilities to pass mail on to the cast, some of whom were in the series ten years ago. So, here's an updated list of the principal stars and main guests and their agent's mail addresses in Australia:

CAROL BURNS
PETA TOPPANO
GLENDA LINSCOTT
PAULA DUNCAN
NIGEL BRADSHAW
PETER HAYES
c/o Kevin Palmer Management
102 Quarry Street
ULTIMO, N.S.W. 2007

ELSPETH BALLANTYNE
SHEILA FLORANCE
PATSY KING
JOY WESTMORE
GERDA NICOLSON
MARY WARD
JULIA BLAKE
BEVERLY DUNN
SANDY GORE
BILLIE HAMMERBERG
LINDA HARTLEY
NIKKI PAUL
JIM SMILLIE
c/o Melbourne Artists Management
643 St. Kilda Road
MELBOURNE, Victoria 3004

PHILIP HYDE
c/o Greaves Laurie Management Ltd
138 Military Road
NEUTRAL BAY, N.S.W. 2089

STEVE KUHN
c/o Fitzgerald-Su Management
15 Randle Street
SURRY HILLS, N.S.W. 2010

GERARD MAGUIRE
BETTY BOBBITT
TOTTIE GOLDSMITH
KATE HOOD
c/o Stacey Testro Management Ltd
153 Park Street (2nd Floor)
SOUTH MELBOURNE, Victoria, 3205

VAL LEHMAN
JANE CLIFTON
LOUISE SIVERSEN
DESIREE SMITH

JILL FORSTER
ANTHONY HAWKINS
c/o Frog Management Ltd
2A Armstrong Street
MIDDLE PARK, Victoria 3206

COLETTE MANN
PETER BENSLEY
IAN GILMOUR
c/o Cameron's Management Ltd
WOOLLOOMOOLOO, N.S.W. 2011

MAGGIE KIRKPATRICK
RICHARD MOIR
c/o Shanahan Management Pty Ltd
129 Bourke Street
WOOLLOOMOOLOO, N.S.W. 2011

KERRY ARMSTRONG
SONJA TALLIS
c/o Barbara Leane Management Ltd
261 Miller Street
NORTH SYDNEY, N.S.W. 2060

AMANDA MUGGLETON
MAGGIE DENCE
SIGRID THORNTON
DIANE CRAIG
LISA CRITTENDEN
SUSANNAH FOWLE
ARIANTHE GALANI
JACKIE WOODBURNE
JULIEANNE NEWBOULD
LES DAYMAN
c/o International Casting Services
147a King Street
SYDNEY, N.S.W. 2000

TINA BURSILL
ROZ SPEIRS

LINDY DAVIES
c/o Robyn Gardiner Management Ltd
P.O. BOX 128
SURRY HILLS, N.S.W. 2010

ANTOINETTE BYRON
LINDA STONER
MAXINE KLIBINGAITIS
RAY MEAGHER
c/o Lee Leslie Management Ltd
72 Glebe Point Road
GLEBE, N.S.W. 2037

KIRSTY CHILD
PAT EVISON
OLIVIA HAMNETT
JUSTINE SAUNDERS
PETER ADAMS
SEAN SCULLY
c/o June Cann Management
6/1 Cnr. Ridge & West Streets
NORTH SYDNEY, N.S.W. 2060

LOIS COLLINDER
JACQUI GORDON
LOUISE LE NAY
PEPE TREVOR
MICHAEL WINCHESTER
c/o Actors' Agency Management
197 Roden Street
WEST MELBOURNE, Victoria 3003

FIONA SPENCE
LESLEY BAKER
ANNE PHELAN
JANET ANDREWARTHA
KYLIE FOSTER
MARGOT KNIGHT
ALETHEA McGRATH

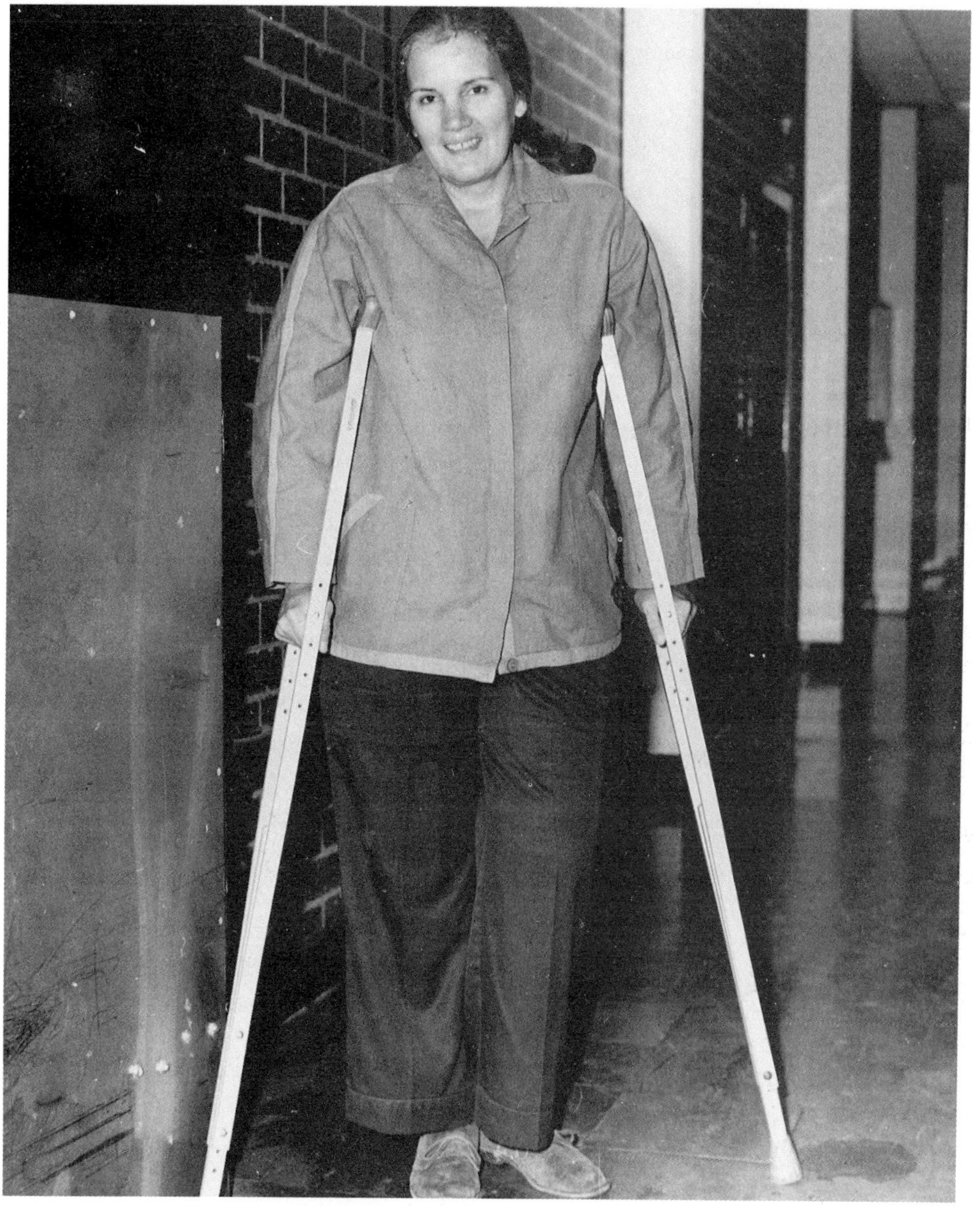

Betty Bobbitt hobbles along the studio corridor on crutches after a slip on the path at home. Writers had to work the mishap into inmate Judy Bryant's storyline for four episodes

MAGGIE MILLAR
c/o Barbara Gange Management
40 Elizabeth Street
NORTH RICHMOND, Victoria 3121

BRIONY BEHETS
VIRGINIA HEY
c/o Anthony Williams Management
50 Oxford Street (1st Floor)
PADDINGTON, N.S.W. 2021

PEPPIE D'OR
c/o JM Casting Services
24 Coleridge Street
ELMWOOD, Victoria 3184

CHRISTINE HARRIS
c/o Bedford & Pearce Pty Ltd
263 Alfred Street (2nd Floor)
NORTH SYDNEY, N.S.W. 2060

ROSANNE HULL-BROWN
c/o The Performers' Management
21 Victoria Street
FITZROY, Victoria 3065

If the actor or actress you wish to write to isn't listed above, send your letter to c/o P.O. Box 229, ST. IVES, N.S.W. 2075, and it will be forwarded on to the addressee.